Marjorie
Engesser

I'M NO DUMMY EVERYDAY
365 Days of Ventriloquial Oddities, Curiosities, and Fun Facts
Copyright © 2021 by Bryan W. Simon. Printed in the United States of America.

Montivagus Press, the imprint of Montivagus Productions, LLC
www.montivaguspress.com

ISBN 978-0-578-85559-2

First Edition 2021

I'M NO DUMMY EVERYDAY

365 Days of Ventriloquial Oddities, Curiosities, and Fun Facts

Bryan W. Simon
with Marjorie Engesser

Montivagus Press the imprint of Montivagus Productions

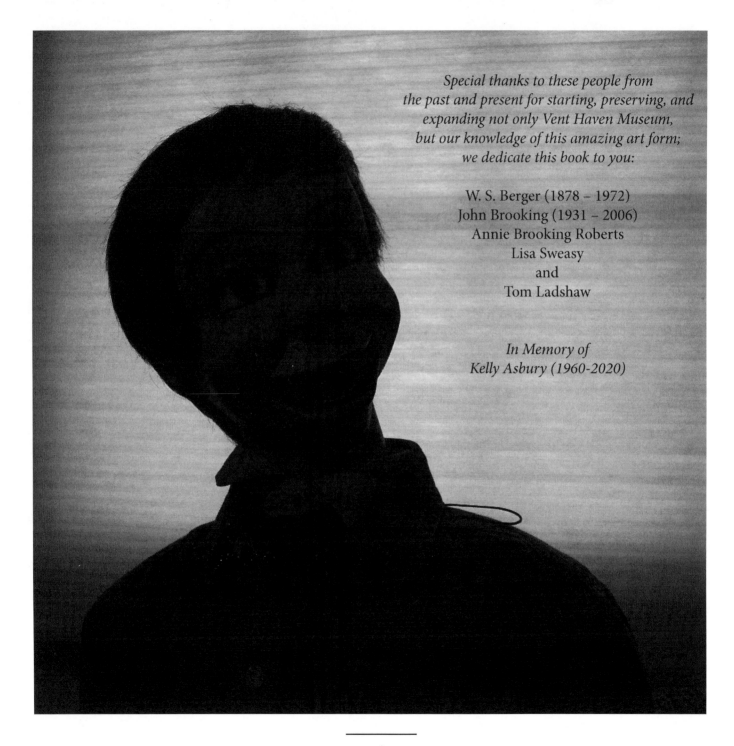

*Special thanks to these people from
the past and present for starting, preserving, and
expanding not only Vent Haven Museum,
but our knowledge of this amazing art form;
we dedicate this book to you:*

W. S. Berger (1878 – 1972)
John Brooking (1931 – 2006)
Annie Brooking Roberts
Lisa Sweasy
and
Tom Ladshaw

*In Memory of
Kelly Asbury (1960-2020)*

V·H·M
VENT HAVEN MUSEUM

Your purchase of this book directly supports VENT HAVEN MUSEUM...

the only museum in the world dedicated to the art of ventriloquism.

Introduction

Writing this book was a lot like making my comedy documentary *I'm No Dummy*, which involved relentless research, constant editing, and tough decisions on what to include and exclude. There were surprises around every corner and constant revelations, all leading to a deeper understanding of this amazing art form. This book is not meant to be a compendium of ventriloquial history, nor a scholarly treatise on the subject, nor a printed version of the film. Instead, its creation is to be informative, entertaining, and enlightening with remarkable facts, legends, myths, stories, and tales passed down by generations of ventriloquists.

Akin to *I'm No Dummy*, I hope this book is a jumping off point.

The inspiration for the book was a simple Facebook page. When *I'm No Dummy* was released, we built a page to promote the film, and it became a repository for photos, clips, news, and trivia that I found interesting. For example, there was "Tuesday Trivia" and "Film Clip Fridays" and, in just a few years, there were nearly 400 entries. And I thought, "Heck, I've done all of this work, so why not put it into some book form." We often posted the birthdays of ventriloquists, so having a calendar book made sense to me. I reached out to Lisa Sweasy, the curator and executive board member at Vent Haven Museum, and executive board member Tom Ladshaw, who was also associate producer on *I'm No Dummy*, and bounced the idea off them. I can't recall if they thought I was nuts or it was a great idea or both. But here we are. Without their never-ending patience, inexhaustible enthusiasm, and helpful gathering of information, you wouldn't be reading this.

Most importantly, I must thank the tireless expertise of film producer Marjorie Engesser, whose editing and design talents were invaluable in making this book come to life.

All profits from this book go directly to Vent Haven Museum; your purchase is a contribution to the only museum in the world dedicated to the art of ventriloquism.

I hope you get a kick out of this as much as I get out of ventriloquism.

Bryan W. Simon
Author and Filmmaker

Foreword

In my twenty years with Vent Haven Museum, I have never met any other non-ventriloquists with such passion for Vent Haven. Bryan and Marge have worked tirelessly on one project after another for the museum's benefit. Their enthusiasm and work ethic are contagious and I've been amazed to watch them take on a daunting task like this book and then see it to conclusion. The museum has been so fortunate to have advocates like Bryan and Marge on our board of advisors and this project is another example of their commitment to our growth and success.

In the pages of this book, you'll find all kinds of trivia and interesting stories about ventriloquists and the art and history of ventriloquism, some dating back centuries and some contemporary. It's been a delight to both research with Bryan and Marge as well as to benefit from their independent research. I've thoroughly enjoyed being a small part of this fun work and I hope each reader enjoys it as well.

As always, our sincere thanks to Bryan and Marge for donating profits from this book to the museum. Vent Haven relies on individuals to support it and we couldn't ask for better friends than Bryan W. Simon and Marge Engesser.

Lisa Sweasy,
Curator, Vent Haven Musem
Executive Board Member

Foreword

This is going to be fun! For the next year, you're going to learn more than you ever imagined about the amazing and wonderful world of... Ventriloquism! No, don't put the book down. You really are going to have fun!

When Bryan W. Simon, a rare individual of boundless energy and endless enthusiasm, mentioned that he would like to take some of the trivia he had learned about ventriloquism and ventriloquists during the making of *I'm No Dummy* and put it into book form, I said, "Bravo!" In fact, I not only said it, I said it without moving my lips!

I met Bryan during the pre-production work on his award-winning documentary film, *I'm No Dummy*. We hit it off and quickly became fast friends and I ultimately ended up playing a much more active role in the production than I would have ever imagined. I recognized in him a true enthusiasm for ventriloquism as an art form. Something about our quirky little universe apparently really spoke to Bryan. Unlike other documentarians who have made films related to ventriloquism and then gone on to the next thing, Bryan has maintained his involvement in the ventriloquial community. He and his wife, Marjorie Engesser, have made numerous trips to Vent Haven Museum and to the annual Vent Haven ConVENTion, as well as spearheaded additional vent related projects. He and Marge have even taken the initiative on their own to host fundraisers for the museum, and as a matter of fact, both Bryan and Marge now serve on the Board of Advisors for Vent Haven Museum.

All of the above should make it obvious that when Bryan Simon announces a new project, you either quickly jump on board or you quickly get out of the way. I am on board!

I love our unusual art form and I love the people involved in it. I especially love their stories. Many of the tales in the ventriloquial community are the stuff of legend. Some stories are well known among ventriloquists, some not so much. My sincere hope is that this book will be a source of fascinating facts and tales for not only our fellow "vents", but for those outside of our little world. I want those "outside" people to learn more about ventriloquism, and in doing so, gain a truly sincere appreciation for those of us with the decidedly unusual occupation of making puppets and other inanimate objects appear to speak and become "living" characters.

I envy you. I already know the stories and bits of trivia you're getting ready to experience. I wish I could discover them all over again. So many of them bring a smile to my face. I sincerely hope they do the same for you while simultaneously deepening your knowledge of and interest in ventriloquism.

Bryan and Marge - - My thanks to you for pushing to make this latest project in the *I'm No Dummy* franchise happen. My thanks to you for insisting that the finished product financially benefit Vent Haven Museum, Inc. My thanks to you for your enthusiasm and never ending advocacy for the vent community. Most of all, my thanks to you for being my friends.

Tom Ladshaw
Executive Board Member

Grace Larsen (Madam Pinxy) Statement
from the 1941 Charter of the
International Brotherhood of Ventriloquists (IBV)

Ventriloquism does not belong to Puppetry, it is one of the kindred arts – closely allied to Magic, conjuration and enchantment. It was cultivated and practiced by Egyptian, Chaldean, Jewish, Roman, and Grecian Priesthoods along with natural magic and used to dupe the ignorant masses, it dates back to the remotest periods of antiquity. Thank goodness both Magic and Ventriloquism are used today for a much finer purpose – of entertainment and to bring laughter and cheer to humanity.

So the logical place for the IBV is associated with the IBM [International Brotherhood of Magicians], who have been most generous in their encouragement and support.

If the members of the IBV will show such enthusiasm, loyalty, friendship and unselfish cooperation to the IBV, as the P. of A. [Puppeteers of America] do for their Organization, then we may hope to grow to be justly recognized and Ventriloquism may take its place as one of the finer arts.

January 1

Ventriloquism was originally a practice used by priests to convince their followers they, the priests, could contact the spirit world. The word comes from the Latin for "to speak from the stomach," i.e. venter (belly) and loqui (speak). The Greeks called this gastromancy. The priests were called Engastrimyths.

In Ancient Greece, people believed that the dead were speaking through the Engastrimyths and that they could translate the noises of the dead into words as well as foretell the future. However, ventriloquists speak from their throat and not their bellies, as the ancient Greeks wrongly believed.

January 2

In 1996, ventriloquist Señor Wences had a street named after him.

He was honored by the City of New York with a blue street sign in Manhattan alongside the Ed Sullivan Theater, designating a block of West 54th Street from Eighth Avenue to Broadway as "Señor Wences Way." He is one of only two ventriloquists to have a street named after him.

VENT HAVEN THE UNOFFICIAL VENTRILOQUISM CAPITAL
OF THE WORLD

WANTED

OLD VENT FIGURES
PHOTOS, PLAYBILLS,
LITHOS, BOOKS, POSTERS
PROGRAMS.
ANYTHING ABOUT VENT.

For sale
Books on ventriloquism
Photos
Send for list

VENT FIGURES
SOLD AND
EXCHANGED

W. S. BERGER, Ventriloquarian

33 West Maple Avenue
Ft. Mitchell-Covington, Ky., U.S.A.

Vent Haven Museum is the only museum in the world dedicated to the art of ventriloquism. Around 1,000 ventriloquial figures are housed there dating back to the American Civil War.

In addition, this repository of ventriloquial history also preserves photos, books, posters, film, sound, and ephemera. Located in Fort Mitchell, Kentucky near Cincinnati, Vent Haven began as a private collection of its founder William Shakespeare Berger (May 13, 1878 – June 24, 1972).

January 4

Happy Birthday to Swedish ventriloquist Cecilia "Zillah" Ustav. Acclaimed as a family entertainer, Zillah was the winner of the first season of *Sweden's Got Talent!* Since then she has hosted four seasons of her own TV show called *APTV med Zillah & Totte* on the major Swedish television network TV4.

Zillah & Totte have released two albums, *Det låter apa* and *Totte (G) apar igen*. She continues touring with her family entertainment comedy show all over Europe along with her monkey partner Totte.

January 5

Today is ventriloquist Dale Brown's birthday. The Wisconsin native has appeared at the MGM Grand in Las Vegas and countless other venues across the country.

Dubbed "the corporate ventriloquist," Dale has authored numerous articles on how to effectively use humor to improve business communications and has written books on the use of ventriloquism as a serious communication tool.

Did you know that there was a guild for ventriloquists' dummies?

In 1951, George McAthy, ventriloquist, magician, and author, started the Brotherhood of Ventriloquists Dummies, a registry, to help prevent duplicating puppet names. At the International Brotherhood of Ventriloquists (IBV) conventions, the figures posed for their own photo without their human partners.

Paul Winchell was one of the great
innovators of ventriloquism by getting
the puppet off the knee. He used
two puppeteers, Jay Lloyd (pictured)
and Skip Ludwig, to help him animate
the figure so he could create separation.
Paul utilized blue screen technology or
chroma keying, as it is commonly
called, to hide himself and his
puppeteers behind the puppet in his
Winchell-Mahoney Time TV series,
which ran from 1965 to 1968.

January 8

Can you match the language with its name for ventriloquism?
Some of them you'll find referenced in this book.

A.	Finnish	1.	ventriloquist
B.	Arabic	2.	ventriloquus
C.	Greek	3.	fukuwa
D.	French	4.	ventriloque
E.	English	5.	buikaprecker
F.	Japanese	6.	vatsastapuhuja
G.	Danish	7.	hasbeszélő
H.	Italian	8.	venilikok'ist
I.	German	9.	engastrmythos
J.	Dutch	10.	brichomluvel
K.	Hungarian	11.	bugtaler
L.	Czech	12.	buktalare
M.	Swedish	13.	ventriloquo
N.	Russian	14.	vantrilok
O.	Latin	15.	bauchrader
P.	Turkish	16.	chrevoveshchatel
Q.	Yiddish	17.	ventrilokvist
R.	Armenian	18.	al-motakallmo min batnihi

Answers: A.6 B.18 C.9 D.4 E.1 F.3 G.11 H.13 I.15
J.5 K.7 L.10 M.12 N.16 O.2 P.14 Q.17 R.8

One of the most amazing music hall and vaudeville ventriloquists was the brilliant Englishman Walter Hibbert Lambert. Lambert was a "protean ventriloquist" and quick-change artist who portrayed multiple characters with multiple figures. One of his most popular personas was Lydia Dreams, a woman.

He also created his own figures, props, costumes, and scenery. Some of Lambert's plays were *Lucky Nutty Jones* (see February 23), *Like Life or The Great Delusion*, *Artistic Artist*, *Grandfather*, and *His Own Grandfather*.

January 10

On this day in 2009, Jay Johnson's first partner Squeaky, along with Spaulding, arrived at Vent Haven Museum. Spaulding appeared in Jay's Tony® Award winning Broadway show, *Jay Johnson: The Two And Only!*, and is displayed in a custom arm/hand modeled after Jay's. The arm/hand that represents Jay holding Spaulding was made by The Mannequin Gallery in Los Angeles.

Did you know that English ventriloquist Thomas Haskey (born 1768) forever changed the public's perception of ventriloquism when he made his debut at London's Sadler's Wells Theatre in 1796?

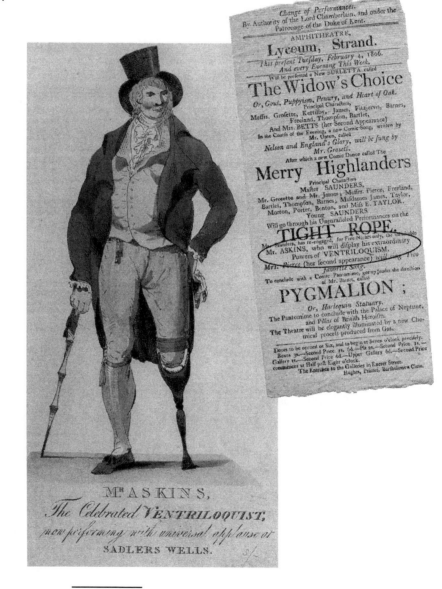

Mr ASKINS,
The Celebrated VENTRILOQUIST,
now performing with universal applause at
SADLERS WELLS.

Appearing as Joseph Askins, he was called, "a wonderful ventriloquistic phenomenon," by the London newspaper *The Oracle and Public Advertiser.* Askins advertised his act as "curious ad libitum" and was sometimes called "The man with one leg and two voices." He utilized a hanky over one hand as his puppet. Askins' performances at Sadler's Wells were on a proscenium stage and, until this time, ventriloquism had only been seen in open-air markets and fairs.

Paul Stadelman (January 12, 1900 – March 17, 1971) was born on this day in 1900. Stadelman was an enthusiastic educator of ventriloquism and also founded Vent-O-Rama at the Abbott Magic Get Together, held annually each summer.

He wrote several educational books on the subject and taught ventriloquism at the Central YMCA in Chicago. The *American* newspaper said it was the first class to be taught to a large group. His "college" course was touted by the *Associated Press, United Press International,* and *ABC Television.*

January 13

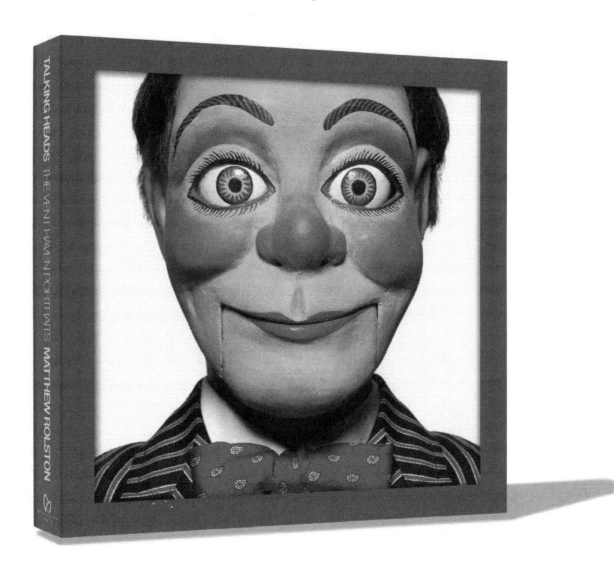

On this day in 2013, Matthew Rolston's book, *Talking Heads: The Vent Haven Portraits*, was published by Pointed Leaf Press. The 224-page portrait book presents an amazing array of figures from Vent Haven Museum, picturing them in a new and illuminating artistic light.

FINIS

Mayann Robinson

ANNAMAY

Did you know that renowned figure maker Finis Henry Robinson, Jr. and his wife Annamay wrote and published two very important books? They were *The Encyclopedia of Lessons in Puppetry* and *The Modern Encyclopedia of Lessons in Ventriloquism*. His parents named him "Finis" (Latin for "the end" or "finished") because he was the last male born in his family.

Did you know that today is the birthday of *I'm No Dummy* alum Kelly Asbury (January 15, 1960 - June 26, 2020)?

Kelly not only appeared in *I'm No Dummy*, but was the first interview for the comedy documentary and opened the door to other interviewees. He also wrote the book, *Dummy Days*, about the golden age of ventriloquism. In addition, Kelly was the two-time Academy Award® nominated director of *Spirit: Stallion of the Cimarron,* and *Shrek 2.*

Vent Haven Museum has around 750 hours of visual media and recordings in their library and archives. 150 of those hours are every second of performance and interview footage that was shot for the documentary, *I'm No Dummy*.

January 17

Did you know that today is the birthday of Phyllis Naomi Hurwitz, better known to all of us as Shari Lewis (January 17, 1933 – August 2, 1998)?

If it weren't for Shari, there wouldn't have been Lamb Chop. Shari is the most recognizable female ventriloquist that ever lived.

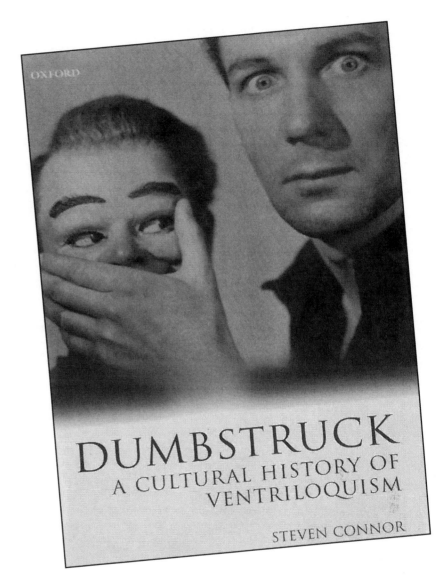

*Dumbstruck: A Cultural History of
Ventriloquism* by Steven Connor
was published on this day in 2001.
Dumbstruck is a wide-ranging,
thoughtful history of ventriloquism
and the disembodied voice. Connor's
philosophical and psychological
observations on the problems,
bewilderment, joy, and absurdities of
the ventriloquial voice speaks loudly to
our contemporary social conditions.

With the advent of variety television, just one appearance on a program like *The Ed Sullivan Show,* *The Hollywood Palace,* or the *Cavalcade of Stars* or a talk show such as *The Tonight Show* or *The Mike Douglas Show* could change the trajectory of a ventriloquist's career. A *Variety* article dated January 18, 1956, entitled, "Get That TV Showcase: Ventro's Fee Zooms" noted that on the strength of his first appearance on *The Ed Sullivan Show,* Rickie Layne went from making $350.00 a week in clubs to $1500.00 a week. That would be almost $20,000.00 a week today.

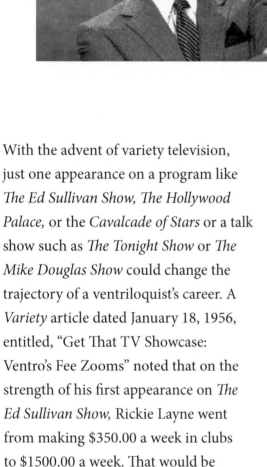

January 20

Terry Fator's ventriloquism career started when he was 10-years-old. While researching a school assignment, he came across a book about ventriloquism entitled, *Ventriloquism for Fun and Profit* by Paul Winchell.

Terry studied the book and learned about the art. A few weeks later, he purchased a Willie Talk dummy, practiced, and won a $25 prize for a performance at a church picnic.

Did you know that the earliest visual record of a ventriloquist was in 1753?

William Hogarth's engraving *An Election Entertainment* depicts ventriloquist Sir John Parnell speaking via his hand.

It was in the 1700s that ventriloquism shifted from sorcery to entertainment. Sir John Parnell's method continued into modern ventriloquial times as Señor Wences used a similar technique to bring alive his partner Johnny as did Jay Marshall with Lefty.

January 22

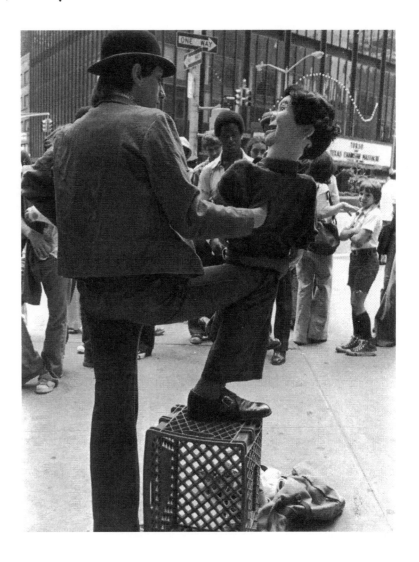

Otto Petersen's partner George has the distinction of being the only puppet to have been assaulted with a deadly weapon.

During a show in Central Park, George's irreverent and nasty comments were taken too seriously by an onlooker, who pulled a knife and stabbed George in the chest multiple times. Otto's hand was inside George and so it was cut, leaving him bloody. Otto wrapped his hand and the duo continued to perform as the police chased George's assailant.

Did you know in the 1930s that Edgar Bergen was grossing $400,000 a year from merchandising his characters? Which is well over six million dollars a year today. As the story goes, Walt Disney convinced Edgar that he would make more from merchandising than performing and that he should copyright his figures.

The only character that surpassed Charlie McCarthy in earnings was none other than Mickey Mouse.

January 24

On this day in 2011, Jimmy Nelson was interviewed about his 70+ years career at Mike Lacey's Comedy and Magic Club in Hermosa Beach, California. Hosted by Tom Ladshaw, and filmed over two days, the shoot was directed by Bryan W. Simon and produced by Marjorie Engesser for their Montivagus Productions. All of the footage from the three cameras was donated to Vent Haven Museum to become part of the media library.

On this day in 1949, at the Hollywood Athletic Club in Los Angeles, a ventriloquist won the very first Emmy® Award . Shirley Dinsdale won for "Outstanding Television Personality" for her children's television show, *Judy Splinters* (KTLA). She was still an undergrad at UCLA at the time and the award was given jointly to both her and her puppet. Shirley was also nominated for "Most Popular Television Program," but did not win.

Arthur Prince moved ventriloquism in a new
direction when he brought a unique style and
simple elegance to his performance.

Prince combined the theatricality of the multiple puppet scenario or playlet with the reality and
intimacy of the single figure partnership. His carefully crafted sketch called *Insubordination* took place
in front of a backdrop of a battleship at sea with only Prince and his figure Sailor Jim. In Great Britain,
it is illegal to wear an authentic military uniform on stage so Prince had to wear a close approximation.

In 1925, The Great Lester performed a stunning piece of ventriloquial showmanship by accident. He was appearing at the Balaban & Katz Theater in Chicago when a crazy trick was played on him. One of Lester's most famous routines was to drink from a glass as his partner Frank Byron, Jr. said, "Going, going, gone."

One night, the musicians substituted full strength whiskey in his decanter, and Lester downed the full glass. Lester's partner, Frank, began sputtering, coughing, and choking; yet not a muscle moved on Lester's face. With that, the 40-member orchestra rose and cheered in a standing ovation.

January 28

According to ventriloquiarian Tom Ladshaw, if you don't know who created a hand carved puppet, one of the best ways to determine who built it is to look at the ears. Tom has identified countless figures for collectors around the world. Heads are sometimes altered, and bodies are often interchanged or replaced. The ears stay the same. Can you match the ear to the figure maker?

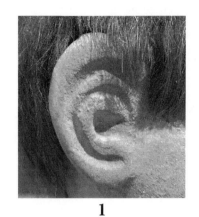

1

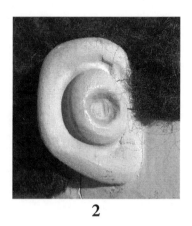

2

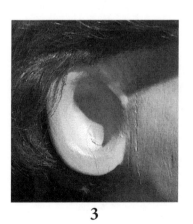

3

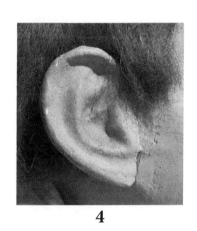

4

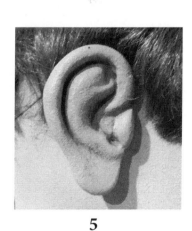

5

Answers: 1. Frank Marshall   2. J. C. Turner   3. Ken Spencer   4. Len Insull Sr.   5. McElroy Brothers

January 29

Early in his career, Jimmy Nelson often worked clubs where the staff was shady. To avoid dressing room theft, he devised a clever way to hide his valuables. Jimmy put his wallet, keys, and watch inside Farfel's body. He figured if anyone tried to get his valuables, Farfel would bite them.

Did you know that today is the birthday of ventriloquist stripper Evelyn West (January 30, 1921 – November 14, 2004)? She was billed as Evelyn "$50,000 Treasure Chest" West, aka the original Hubba Hubba Girl. Evelyn wanted to change up her act in the 1940s and since she often worked with headlining ventriloquist Phil D'Rey, she had him coach her in the art of ventriloquism. As Evelyn and her figure Esky would chat and dance around the stage, she would remove more and more of her clothing.

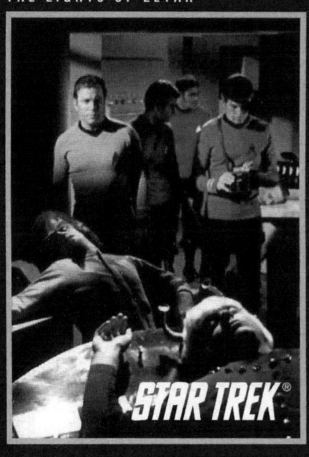

STAR TREK

"THE LIGHTS OF ZETAR"

Written by

Jeremy Tarcher

and

Shari Lewis

Prod. #60043-73
Series Created by
Gene Roddenberry
Paramount TV Productions

FINAL DRAFT

October 28, 1968

(c) Copyright 1968 by PARAMOUNT PICTURES CORPORATION
and NORWAY CORPORATION
All rights reserved.

Did you know that the multi-talented Shari Lewis was a huge fan of science fiction and fantasy? She wrote the Star Trek episode "The Lights of Zetar" with her husband Jeremy Tarcher. It aired today in 1969. Shari wrote the role of Lt. Mira Romaine for herself, but Jan Shutan ended up playing the part in Season 3, Episode 18.

Celebrity Charades was a syndicated game show that premiered on this day in 1979 hosted by Jay Johnson and Squeaky.

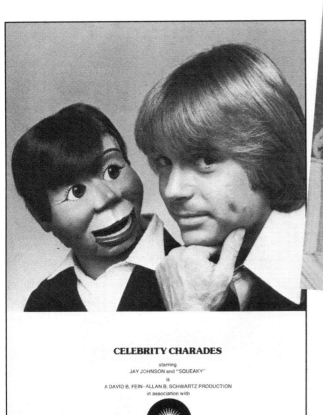

CELEBRITY CHARADES

starring
JAY JOHNSON and "SQUEAKY"
is
A DAVID B. FEIN · ALLAN B. SCHWARTZ PRODUCTION
in association with

Columbia Pictures Television

The show consisted of two teams of four celebrities attempting to act out comedic phrases, each within 75 seconds. The team who guessed all their phrases in the least amount of time won $500 for their favorite charity.

This month in 1955, Nestlé Quik commercials began airing. For over a decade, Jimmy Nelson, Danny O'Day, and Farfel were the spokespersons for Nestlé. The trio made 120+ commercials with their signature singing of the jingle, which became iconic.

February 2

It was this month in 1988 when *Detective Comics (DC)* introduced Arnold Wesker who was known as "The Ventriloquist," one of Batman's super villain enemies. Wesker, a timid man, plans and executes his criminal activities through his 1920s gangster puppet partner, Scarface.

The only copy of a pre-release *I'm No Dummy* poster is at Vent Haven Museum in Fort Mitchell, Kentucky. The poster was inspired by a photograph of dummies preparing to strike.

This original *I'm No Dummy* poster was designed by producer Marjorie Engesser but never displayed. A new poster was designed for the World Premiere in Seattle.

February 4

Before *America's Got Talent*, there was Arthur Godfrey's *Talent Scouts*. Did you know that Shari Lewis won *Talent Scouts* in 1952? Shari would appear two more times on Arthur Godfrey's TV specials in 1963. They were *Arthur Godfrey Loves Animals* and *The Arthur Godfrey Thanksgiving Special*.

SHARI LEWIS
and her
"wood"-be friends
Sampson & Buttercup

SHARI
1505 Archer Rd.
Bronx 62, NY
TA.8-8755

February 5

On this day in 1942, ventriloquist Angel Mignanelli (February 5, 1942 - April 3, 2004) was born. Her stage names included Angela Martin, Angele McNeil, Angel Miganel, and just Angel. Angel had been a professional for only six months when at age eight, with her partner Tiny, she made her television debut on Connie Francis' show *Star Time*.

After *Star Time*, Angel played the Roxy and Palace Theaters in NYC and had a twice-weekly television show. By age 19, she was singing, dancing, and performing ventriloquism at the Copacabana. At age 26, she portrayed "The Ventriloquist" and "Ma Templeton" in the original 1968 musical production of *George M* on Broadway.

———

February 6

On this day in 1961, ventriloquist Paul Winchell filed for a patent for his latest invention, an artificial heart. He received the patent, number 3,097,366, on July 16, 1963. He was the first person to build and patent a mechanical artificial heart.

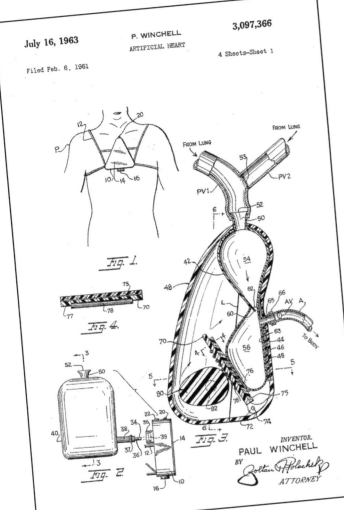

According to the Massachusetts Institute of Technology, Winchell received over 30 patents in his lifetime for such items as a disposable razor, blood plasma defroster, flameless cigarette lighter, "invisible" garter belt, fountain pen with a retractable tip, and battery-heated gloves.

February 7

RONN LUCAS

On this day in 1990, American ventriloquist Ronn Lucas was given his own television show in England. *The Ronn Lucas Show* was a weekly sketch comedy series on Thames TV that lasted five years.

February 8

Edgar Bergen was inducted into the Hollywood Walk of Fame three times for his contributions to television, motion pictures, and radio on this date in 1960.

His three stars were presented on the same day – an honor that has never been duplicated.

February 9

On this day in 1978, *The Ventriloquist's Wife* premiered at the Village Gate Theater, Off-Broadway in New York City. Written, directed, and starring the Ridiculous Theater Company's artistic director Charles Ludlam, the hour long one-act comic thriller is about stand-up comic Charles going nowhere until he buys a vent figure and names him Walter Ego. Charles' wife Susan begins to resent the time her husband spends with his dummy and Walter Ego takes on a murderous life of his own.

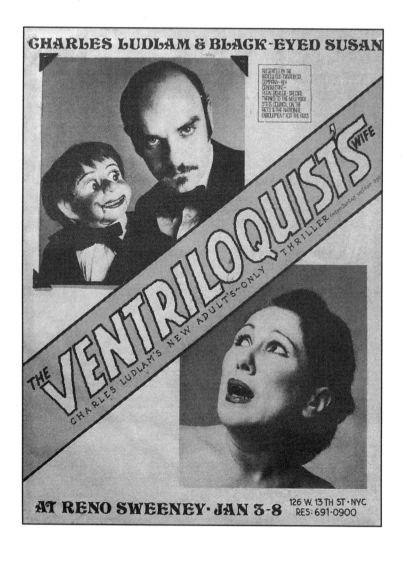

The *New York Times* heralded the play as, "One of Mr. Ludlam's most inspired creations…mesmerizing…high comic art." And the *Village Voice* stated, "A miniature magic psychodrama, a funny but slightly unnerving vision of the nuclear family…pure pleasure." Walter Ego now resides at Vent Haven Museum.

February 10

Ventriloquist Sylvia Cirilo-Fletcher's first children's book entitled, *The Adventures of Sylvie & the Magic Trunk,* was published in 2009 on this day.

It was the first in a series of books about Sylvie, a shy young girl who learns to use her special talent for ventriloquism to make people happy. Sylvia Cirilo-Fletcher's love of performing for children inspired her to write this book and it is based on one of Sylvia's earliest performances in front of her elementary school class. Her second book in the series is called, *Sylvie & The Magic Trunk: Smoulder the Stega-Dragon.*

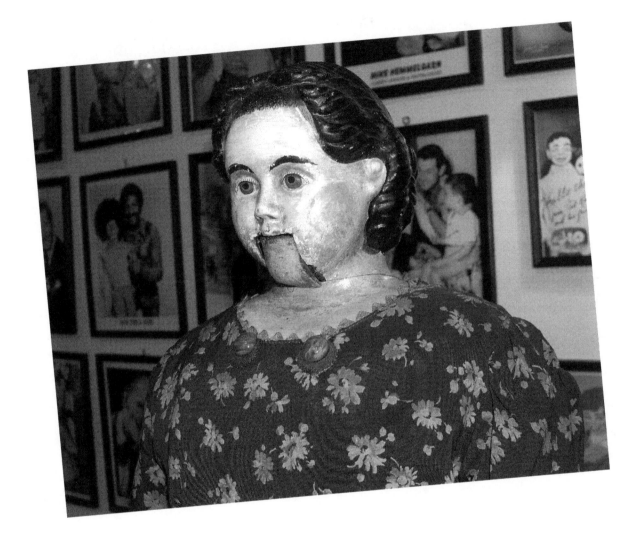

One of the oldest ventriloquial figures housed at Vent Haven Museum arrived on this day in 1944. Hunter Girl, as she is called, was originally a doll for little girls made around 1863 by the Greiner Doll Company. Henry Hunter, a tinsmith and soldier during the Civil War, modified her with a simple mouth movement, using the figure to entertain his friends.

Did you know that today is the birthday of cowboy ventriloquist Max Terhune (February 12, 1891 – June 5, 1973)?

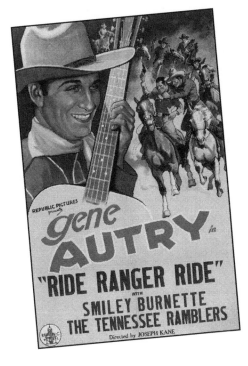

The talented Terhune was also a magician. Card tricks were his specialty, and as a former vaudevillian, he could also juggle, do bird calls, and barnyard animal impressions, often incorporating them into his film and TV performances. Max's first appearance on camera was in the film *Ride, Ranger, Ride* (1936) with Gene Autry. Later, he always appeared on film with his partner, Elmer Sneezeweed. Max had more than one Elmer and the one that resides at Vent Haven Museum was used in his live performances.

February 13

This week on February 16, 1959, Joy Records released a 45-RPM record featuring Señor Wences with the songs "S-All Right? S-All Right" and "Deefeecult For You – Easy For Me." These were the iconic catchphrases used by Señor Wences in his celebrated performances. The songwriting team of Dick Manning and Al Hoffman composed the tunes with James Tyler as the arranger.

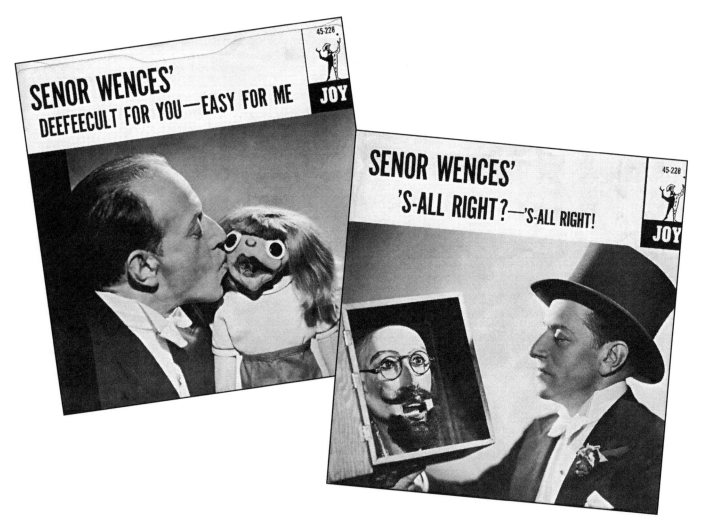

February 14

Happy Valentine's Day!

Did you know that today is the birthday of Elizabeth "Annie" Roberts, member of the Vent Haven Museum Board of Directors and former curator? She was instrumental in helping the *I'm No Dummy* documentary get made.

A great way to show you care about ventriloquism and to celebrate Valentine's Day is by giving a small gift to the museum: *www.venthavenmuseum.org*.

February 15

On this date in 1978, the groundbreaking film *Coming Home* was released. The film was awarded three Oscars®. Willie Tyler portrayed Virgil, a paraplegic Vietnam vet, who was a ventriloquist. His usual puppet partner Lester did not appear in the film but Willie used Lester's voice for his on-screen Vietnamese puppet partner.

Did you know that on this day Edgar Bergen (Edgar John Berggren, February 16, 1903 - September 30, 1978) was born?

Conceivably the most popular ventriloquist of all time, very few ventriloquists were as influential on the art form as Bergen.

February 17

Today is the birthday of
the pioneering ventriloquist
John Walcott Cooper
(February 17, 1873 – April 17, 1966).

Cooper began performing in minstrel shows in
1897, billed as the ventriloquist "Prince Madagascar"
to make him sound more exotic. In 1900 he joined the
Richards and Pringles Minstrels. Cooper broke the
color barrier during the vaudeville era in 1902 when he
was billed as the "Black Napoleon of Ventriloquism."
Cooper was the first Black to perform before white
vaudeville audiences.

February 17

On this date in 1930, through their Vitaphone Studio, Warner Brothers released *The Operation*, a ten-minute short starring Edgar Bergen and Charlie McCarthy. It was Edgar Bergen's first movie and was a filmed version of a skit he and Charlie had performed on countless vaudeville stages. They revived the skit for television, Las Vegas, and road shows.

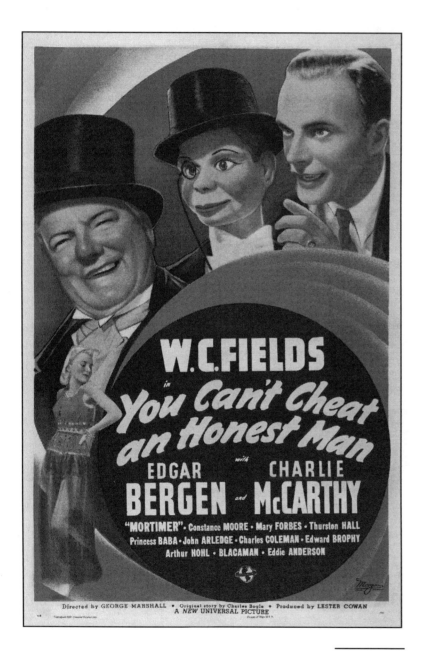

You Can't Cheat An Honest Man with Edgar Bergen, Charlie McCarthy, and W. C. Fields was officially released on this day in 1939.

W. C. Fields became a big hit on radio, especially on Edgar Bergen's radio program, where Fields had a long running "feud" with Charlie McCarthy. This film was an attempt to capitalize on the popularity of that feud. Each morning of filming there would be a cast meeting including Bergen and Charlie. Charlie became so disruptive during these sessions that Fields eventually banned him from attending meetings.

This poster may be viewed in full color at Vent Haven Museum.

On this night in 1908, Will B. Wood, known as the "World's Greatest Ventriloquist," left Frontera, Mexico on a northern voyage through the Gulf to Progresso, Mexico to tour there. Wood and his 20-year-old daughter Bertha had just completed a very successful three-year tour of South America. At about midnight, an unexpected storm caused the tugboat they were on to founder, washing the crew, lifeboats, and cargo overboard. Just nine miles from the Laguna de Terminos lighthouse, Wood and his daughter tried to swim to safety but died of exposure. However several of his puppet partners made it, floating to shore in trunks. Four of them are now safe and sound at Vent Haven Museum.

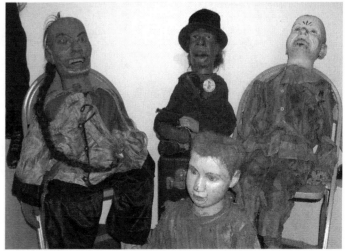

February 19

On this day in 2017, Elliot Anders performed the *I'm No Dummy* opening theme at the Auburn State Theater with a string quartet. Behind the musicians was a large screen on which the film portion was projected. The program entitled *Elliot Anders: A Musical Life* was a retrospective of his original compositions in feature films, documentaries and musical theater.

Elliot composed the original score for *I'm No Dummy* and was the sound designer for the big screen adaptation of *Jay Johnson: The Two & Only!*

February 20

American ventriloquist Valentine Vox was born in
Britain as Jack Kenneth Riley on this day in 1939.
In 1977, he took his stage name from the 1840
Victorian novel, *The Life and Adventures of Valentine
Vox the Ventriloquist* by Henry Cockton.

In 1997, Vox was director of the International Ventriloquist Association and organized
an annual ventriloquists' convention in Las Vegas from 1997 to 2003. He has appeared
at venues around the world including theatre, cabaret, and on television. In addition to
English, Vox has performed his act in Japanese and German.

February 21

Annually, *The Grammy Awards* are presented this month to the best recording artists in the world. Did you know that Paul Winchell is the only ventriloquist to win a Grammy Award? He won "Best Recording for Children" in 1975 for *Winnie the Pooh and Tigger Too.*

February 22

Ventriloquist Taylor Mason was born today.

During his last two years at the University of Illinois, Mason re-discovered a ventriloquist puppet given to him by his parents for a 10th birthday gift. Reviving his skill as a ventriloquist, he combined the puppet, stand-up comedy, and music into a one-man variety show. In 1990, Mason was cast on *Star Search*, hosted by Ed McMahon; he was the grand-prize winner, earning $100,000.

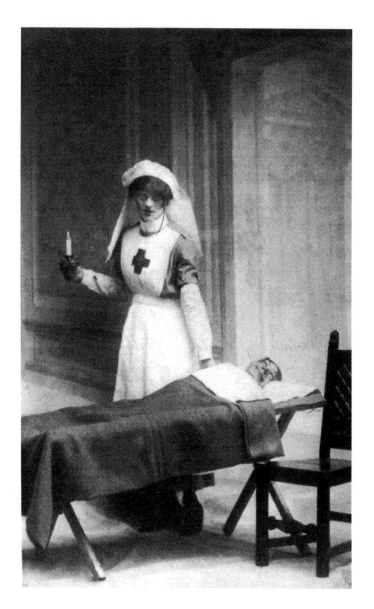

The 1920s saw a boom in the film industry and the clever Walter Hibbert Lambert (see January 9) incorporated this cheap entertainment into one of his most famous productions, called *Lucky Nutty Jones*. The play began with a three-minute movie that ended with a horrible auto accident. As the movie dimmed, the lights came up to reveal a hospital room with Lambert portraying Nurse Rose. She comforted the patient, actually a puppet, who is in bed moaning and writhing. Lambert voiced the patient while his daughter manipulated the figure from under the bed.

A critic stated, "One of the most original and clever ventriloquial acts we have ever seen. It has an end which will surprise those not familiar with it."

The play ended with the nurse pulling off the patient's head. The audience shrieked because they assumed the patient was a real person. Topping this climax, Lambert removed his wig to reveal that he was a man, as the audience cheered.

February 24

Edgar Bergen was the author of the ventriloquism article for the *Encyclopedia Britannica*. It was published in Volume 23, on page 70 of the Fourteenth Edition, ©1948. The author's initials at the end of the article were E.J.Bn for Edgar John Bergen. Bergen began his entry by stating, "Ventriloquism, the art of producing voice in such a manner that it shall appear from some other place altogether distant from the speaker (Lat. Veneter, belly, loqui, to speak)."

Today is the birthday of ventriloquist Ronn Lucas. He has starred in his own TV variety series, performed before United States presidents, guest-starred on television, and was the first ventriloquist to have his own, long-running show in Las Vegas. Among Ronn's many accomplishments is his performance in the Broadway show *Sugar Babies* with Mickey Rooney and Ann Miller. He performed in the show from 1981 through 1982, and then again in the National Tour through 1983. He is even on the original cast album.

February 26

Did you know that today is the birthday of British ventriloquist Peter Brough (February 26, 1916 – June 3, 1999)? In 1950, Peter and his partner Archie debuted their radio series *Educating Archie*. The show moved to television in 1958.

The radio show averaged 15 million listeners per week, and at its peak, had 25,000 members in its fan club.

February 27

Today in 2002, Donald Earl "Don" Messick's (September 7, 1928 – October 24, 1997) figure Woody DeForrest arrived at Vent Haven Museum.

When he started out in show business, Don supported himself as a ventriloquist, but soon found his way into voice acting in animation. Don performed 412 characters on 172 titles almost exclusively for Hanna-Barbera. His most famous voices were Scooby-Doo, Dr. Benton Quest, Boo Boo Bear, and Bamm-Bamm Rubble, to name just a few.

February 28

It was on this day in 1992 that the TV series *Scorch* premiered on the CBS Network. Based on Ronn Lucas' dragon puppet partner, Scorch was 1,300-years-old and lived with a TV weatherman and his daughter. Scorch appeared with the weatherman on a news program posing as a ventriloquist dummy. Ronn was the puppeteer, voice, and writer on the series.

February 29 (Leap Year Edition)

Ventriloquist Fred Ketch was a prolific cartoonist and his cartoons populated the pages of the International Brotherhood of Ventriloquists (IBV) magazine, *The Oracle*. Fred had his own distinct style and his cartoons were also seen in various magazines and journals. He would also send cartoon postcards to his friends and fans to keep in touch.

February 31

On this fictitious day in 1924 the Great Lester's partner, Frank Byron, Jr., was arrested for stealing laughs in Detroit, Michigan. Many ventriloquists have attempted to give the illusion that their puppet partners have a life outside of the act. The Great Lester constructed one of the most unbelievable. The record also shows that he "has a wonderful way with the ladies." It doesn't appear that he served any time, other than his time on stage.

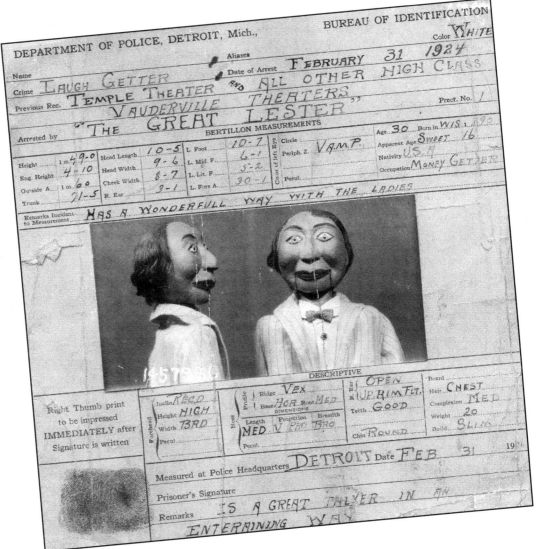

March 1

This week in 2003, *Dummy* won the Special Jury Award at the Santa Barbara Film Festival. The film starred Academy® Award winner Adrien Brody as Steven, a down on his luck, unemployed office worker who takes up ventriloquism after seeing Edgar Bergen in *You Can't Cheat an Honest Man.*

Brody performed all of the ventriloquism and puppet manipulation, after intensive coaching from *I'm No Dummy* alum Alan Semok. For the film Semok portrayed Professor Parlepancia and had already created and designed Brody's vent partner who resides at Vent Haven Museum. Paul Winchell was a Special Technical Advisor.

In March of 2007, *Detective Comics* introduced a female version of "The Ventriloquist." Her name was Peyton Riley and, unlike Arnold Wesker in the 1988 version of "The Ventriloquist," Peyton believed she and her figure, also named Scarface, were in a committed relationship. Scarface called her "Sugar."

The Vent Event was broadcast on this day in 1978. Everybody knows HBO, but in 1978 they were a fledgling cable company less than six years old, and they wanted to produce original programming. *The Vent Event* was one of their first. Steve Allen hosted the show and some of the ventriloquists who appeared were: Edgar Bergen, Lou Dupont, Jay Johnson, Shari Lewis, Jimmy Nelson, Jim Teter, and Willie Tyler. This was one of the last times Jay would appear with Squeaky as his regular partner.

———

March 4

On this day in 1937, at the 9th annual *Academy® Awards*, the Academy of Motion Picture Arts and Sciences presented an honorary Academy® Award to Edgar Bergen and Charlie McCarthy. The statuette was in the traditional shape of the Oscar®, but carved from wood and with a moving mouth so Bergen could make it talk.

George (Professor Pinxy) Larsen (1886 – 1960) was a figure maker who carved the individualized figures he and his wife, Grace (Madam Pinxy, 1883 - 1948), used when they performed. Grace handmade all the clothes for them from their small workshop on the north side of Chicago.

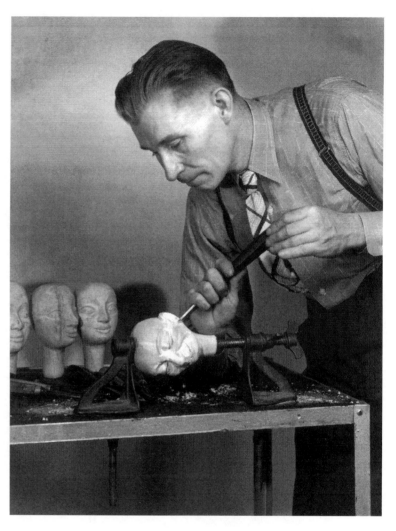

As a member of the Chicago Carvers and Craftsmen, George Larsen was featured in the December 1939 issue of *Popular Science*, which highlighted the fact that performers throughout the world used his figures. Not limited to figure making, Larsen was also a tattoo artist with a studio on Navy Pier in Chicago.

March 6

The East Coast premiere of *I'm No Dummy* at the New York International Children's Film Festival was on this day in 2010. After the sold out performance, Tom Ladshaw, Lynn Trefzger, and Jay Johnson held a workshop for all of the attendees.

Participants received their own take home sock puppet and *The Almost Instant Ventriloquism* instructional book written by Tom Ladshaw. The cover of the book was a variation of the never displayed original *I'm No Dummy* poster (see February 3rd).

March 7

This week in 1993, Lamb Chop became the first and only ventriloquial figure to testify before Congress. Here is a portion of her testimony:

Miss Lamb Chop: Mr. Chairman, I would like to know, am I on my own time, or do I get only part of Shari's?

Rep. Edward Markey, D-Mass., Chairman House Telecommunications Subcommittee: You get your own time, Miss Lamb Chop.

Miss Lamb Chop: Thank you, sir.

Miss Lamb Chop [To Shari Lewis]: ...if you want to interrupt, lift your hand. Your left hand.

Mr. Chairman, I have been entertaining children for 35 years, which is a long time in the life of a 6 year old. I would like to say that we really need your help and your care and concern, and we need the best that you grown-ups have to offer. And if you give it to us, we will give the good stuff back. Not only to you, but to our own children as well.

March 8

Happy Birthday to *I'm No Dummy* alum and one of the finest ventriloquists out there, Lynn Trefzger. An extremely talented and innovative ventriloquist who's always in demand, Lynn has performed all over the world, on land and sea.

March 9

Did you know that today is the birthday of revered figure maker Frank Marshall (March 9, 1900 – October 10, 1969)?

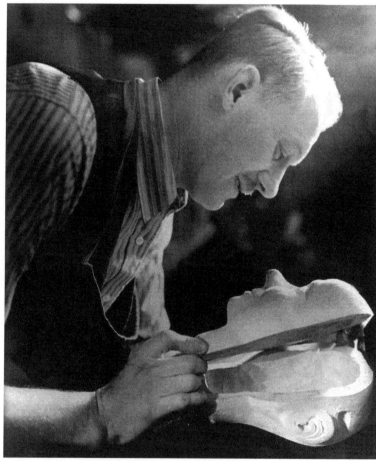

Born Frank Marzalkiewicz, he carved many of the famous figures during the Golden Age of ventriloquism. He was without a doubt one of the most influential figure makers in the history of ventriloquism.

March 10

Fred Maher, along with his wife Madeleine, opened Maher Ventriloquist Studios in Detroit, Michigan, advancing the art form of ventriloquism. Maher's advertising listed the beginning of the school as 1934. The thrust of the business was a home study course called "The Maher Course of Ventriloquism" which was copyrighted in 1942.

Ventriloquism was not widely taught until Maher started this simple home study course which could be financed by the GI bill. There were a few teachers here and there, and how-to-books, but the Mahers changed everything as thousands of students over the years purchased the course, many going on to be successful professionals. Maher promised, "Anyone can learn."

March 11

Nina Conti's film, *Her Master's Voice*, had its world premiere on this date in 2012 at the South by Southwest Film Festival in Austin, Texas. It went on to win the Audience Award in SXGlobal.

In this mockumentary, Nina takes the bereaved puppets of her mentor and erstwhile lover (Ken Campbell) on a pilgrimage to the Vent Haven ConVENTion for their final resting place. She gets to know her latex and wooden travelling partners along the way, and with them, deconstructs herself and her lost lover. This film is truly unique in genre and style.

March 12

Family Tree, the HBO television series, premiered on this date in 2013. Nina Conti portrays family member Bea Chadwick, a ventriloquist who believes her puppet Monk is real.

March 13

Did you know that Jimmy Nelson was featured in a *Jeopardy* answer/question on this day in 1999?

WORD THAT COMPLETES
THE LINE SUNG
BY JIMMY NELSON
"N-E-S-T-L-E-S, NESTLE'S
MAKES
THE VERY BEST...?"

The Answer:

Word that completes the line sung by Jimmy Nelson "N-e-s-t-l-e-s, Nestlé's makes the very best...?"

The Question:

What is Chocolate?

Did you know that today is Finnish ventriloquist Sari Aalto's birthday? In Finnish a ventriloquist is called a "vatsastapuhuja" or a stomach speaker. In 2016 Sari placed second on the *Talent Finland* television program, and in 2018 she made her American debut at the Vent Haven International Ventriloquist ConVENTion.

The word "dummy" did not mean "substitute for a real thing or a model of a human being" until the mid 1800s. In England, dummy means a baby's pacifier so they call them ventriloquial dolls. Many ventriloquists will not use the word "dummy" because of its Old English/Germanic origin around 1200 AD which meant "mute, silent, refraining from speaking or unable to speak" because they believe that their partners can speak.

The Vent Haven Museum has hundreds of posters, playbills, and flyers from all over the world in their library and archives. This German poster states:

Stage Performance
Alfred Kühn
cheerful dialogues with "Anton"
Saxony's most original ventriloquist
"Alfredo"
Art, Humor and Satire accompanied by
concert zither

(continued)

Many of the posters and playbills in the museum's library date back to the early 1800s.

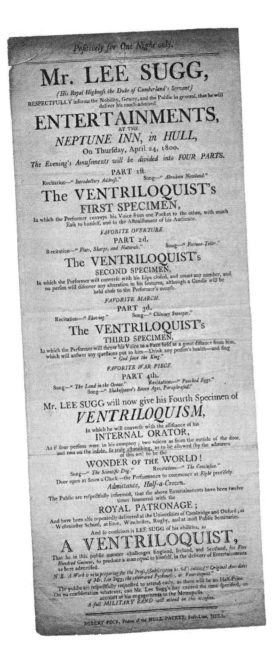

March 17

Rumor has it that Max Terhune's partner, Elmer, quit drinking and smoking once he arrived at Vent Haven Museum.

March 18

Brothers Glenn and George McElroy from Harrison, Ohio, were arguably among the finest figure makers in the ventriloquial art form. Although the two of them made very few figures, Vent Haven Museum has eight plus several figures the brothers did extensive work on.

When the highly regarded figure maker Frank Marshall saw a McElroy figure in 1938 he said: "I have to take my hat off to these boys. Looks like I will have to go out of business."

(continued)

March 19

The McElroy brothers are revered for their imaginative and intricate figures prized by many ventriloquists and collectors, but their figure making careers only lasted from 1936 to 1941. In 1965 they came out of retirement to make one more figure for an ABC Television producer. They became founding members of the Vent Haven Museum Board of Advisors in 1973.

Even their logo illustrated their unique talents in figure making.

March 20

This week in 1927, young American ventriloquist Edgar Bergen, made his debut in England at London's Holborn Theatre in a ten-minute skit entitled, "The Operation."

Charlie McCarthy was not the sophisticated Charlie that was so common later on; he was portrayed as a smart aleck Irish newspaper boy. Vitaphone actually turned the skit into a short film (See February 17).

March 21

In the late 1700s through the early 1800s, the well-known ventriloquist Le Sieur Thiemet, known as "Imitator and Physiomane," regaled the likes of Napoleon and Josephine as well as other noble and prominent Europeans with his distant noises and voices performances.

He would reproduce in detail and without facial gesture, a foxhunt as heard by a person locked inside a country mill, conveying the sounds of French horns in the distance, horses galloping, voices of the hunters, and the hounds in full cry as they passed and faded away in the night. Soon a rooster crowed and the conversation of the miller and the gentleman in his mill ended the scene.

Did you know that The Great Lester's vent partner, Frank Byron, Jr., resides at Vent Haven Museum? The museum also has Lester's teaching board, a costume of Lester's, his prop phone, his stage makeup kit, hundreds of photos, and his personal correspondence file in their archives. Lester made Frank Byron, Jr. himself under the watchful eye of Theodore Mack around 1902.

March 23

On this day in 1966, Paul Winchell guest starred on *The Dick Van Dyke Show* with Snitchy the Snail, a puppet he rarely used.

Paul requested that his puppet have a character name like any other actor on the show so Snitchy became Jelly Bean. Entitled "Talk to the Snail," this episode featured Claude Wilbur (Winchell) who is partnered with the mean and irritable Jelly Bean. Wilbur and Jelly Bean are interviewing Rob Petrie (Dick Van Dyke) to be the head writer of their new kids' television show.

March 24

Did you know that Bob Evans' partner Jerry O'Leary, who now resides at Vent Haven, had a girlfriend?

Here's a quote from a 1940s photo spread from a Minneapolis, Minnesota newspaper: "When Bob Evans, ventriloquist, arrived in town with his partner Jerry O'Leary to appear in Hotel Nicollet's Minnesota Terrace, Jerry immediately proceeded to renew acquaintances with his dummy lady-friend, Suzanne, a radio controlled doll owned by the Arthur Murray Studio." I wonder who paid for dinner?

Buddy Big Mountain is not only an accomplished
ventriloquist, but also a renowned master marionettist.
With his puppet Stumbling Bear, Buddy shares
the knowledge of his rich Native American heritage.

March 26

After World War II, no company had a greater impact on the advancement of ventriloquism than the Juro Novelty Company.

SPOTLIGHT YOUR SALES!

with

Edgar Bergen and Jimmy Nelson

JURO's
cast of
celebrity dolls

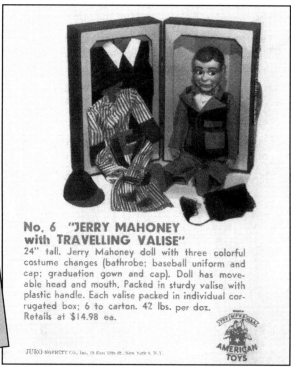

No. 6 "JERRY MAHONEY with TRAVELLING VALISE"
24" tall. Jerry Mahoney doll with three colorful costume changes (bathrobe; baseball uniform and cap; graduation gown and cap). Doll has moveable head and mouth. Packed in sturdy valise with plastic handle. Each valise packed in individual corrugated box; 6 to carton. 42 lbs. per doz. Retails at $14.98 ea.

AMERICAN TOYS

JURO NOVELTY CO., Inc. 18 East 18th St., New York 3, N. Y.

Founded by Sam Jupiter in the late 1940s, Juro manufactured ventriloquist puppets for girls and boys – Paul Winchell's Jerry Mahoney was their first. More followed as Juro teamed up with Rickie Layne to produce a Velvel puppet. Jimmy Nelson's Danny O'Day and Farfel puppets were introduced at the New York Toy Fair in 1963. Juro later added Charlie McCarthy, Mortimer Snerd, and Willie Tyler's Lester.

March 27

On this date in 2010 the MTV series *Victorious* premiered. Centered on a group of students who attend the fictional Hollywood Arts High School, Robbie, played by Matt Bennett, is a ventriloquist who has a puppet named Rex that accompanies him everywhere.

Bennett was coached by Tony® Award winning ventriloquist Jay Johnson and the two developed Rex's character. In an interview, Bennett stated that his figure, "...talks for me, he does everything Robbie wants, and says what Rob is feeling because Rob himself is very insecure and he really helps him get through hard times."

March 28

Charlie, Herbert Dexter's partner, is the only puppet to be named co-respondent in a divorce.

In 1932, the newly married blues singer Sally Osman and ventriloquist Dexter developed a stage act together. When the dummy began to interrupt her songs with cruel ad libs and rob her of applause by making rude wise-cracks, Osman asked Dexter to change the act so that she could sing without interruption. He refused.

(continued)

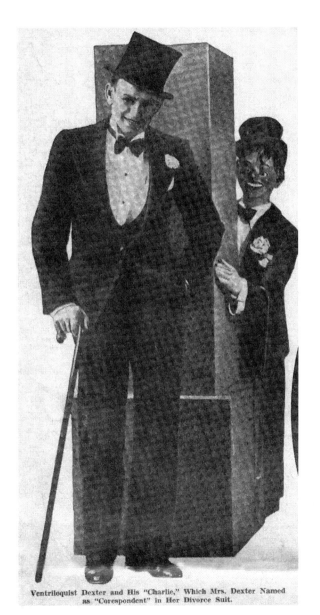

Ventriloquist Dexter and His "Charlie," Which Mrs. Dexter Named as "Corespondent" in Her Divorce Suit.

Osman testified in the 1934 case, "I got to hate Charlie so deeply that homicidal thoughts began to haunt my mind." When the judge asked why she hadn't requested alimony, she said, "I wouldn't be able to collect it anyway; he spends all his money on Charlie." Dexter never contested the proceedings and Osman got her divorce.

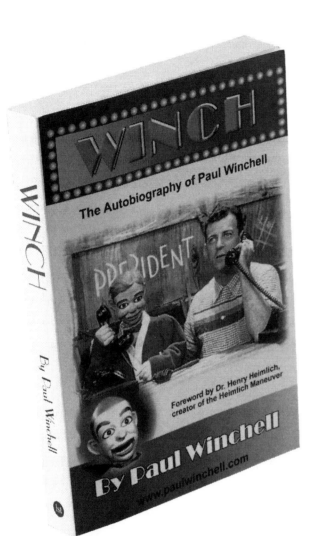

Winch, Paul Winchell's autobiography, was published on this date in 2004.

"Winch...is not a typical Hollywood memoir. In fact, it is more like a Twilight Zone episode, in which a celebrity ventriloquist and television star, Paul Winchell lives out his life in two totally separate worlds. Winch, despite his great success, lives in a supernatural [emotional] world, assailed by an apparition, which assumes monstrous, almost deific proportions."

Edgar Bergen, Frank Marshall and the workings of a figure's head were featured in the March 1938 issue of *Popular Mechanics*.

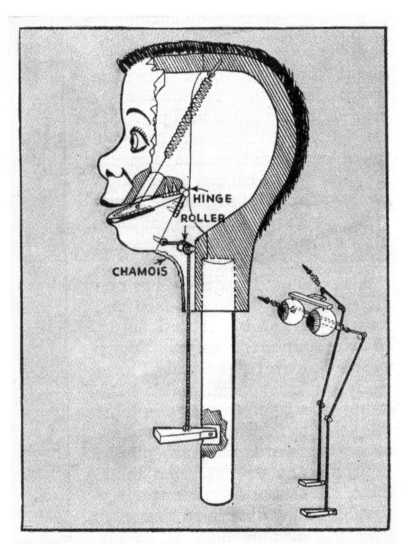

In the article entitled, "Radio Revives An Ancient Art," a sketch of Edgar Bergen's partner Charlie McCarthy, illustrated how the eyes and mouth are manipulated by the ventriloquist. This is an aspect of the art form that is rarely shared with the public.

April 1

British-born Maude Edwards (1886-1976) is considered the first great female ventriloquist. She made her stage debut in 1905, trained and managed by her older brother, Tom Edwards, who was also a ventriloquist.

Edwards and her partner Nobbler, a stable boy figure, went to the United States in October 1906, where she toured American Music Halls until May 1907. Upon her return from a successful tour, she decided her brother was taking too large a slice of her earnings and sued him in the High Court. She won her case.

April 2

Did you know that today is the birthday of the great ventriloquist Jules Vernon (April 2, 1867 – May 17, 1937)?

Born Walter Lester Pope Knyvett, Vernon came to the United States from Great Britain in 1885 at the age of 18. One of the finest ventriloquists of the time, his signature act was set in a hotel lobby and involved as many as 18 puppet characters such as a bellhop, a house detective, guests, and an elevator operator who kept saying, "Going Up?" He operated some puppets manually, some via pneumatic hoses, and others with foot pedals. Tragically, Vernon went blind suddenly on Christmas morning, 1920.

(continued)

April 3

Vernon was a creative ventriloquist and continued to travel and perform, never revealing to any of his audiences that he was blind. As the story goes, he supposedly achieved this by having his wife Minnie mount the puppets together on a bench, which were connected to a black thread running from backstage. Vernon followed the thread to the bench, and, knowing where each control was, performed as though he could see. Instead of using 18 figures, now he used seven, which were operated with nine strings, an air bulb and one foot pedal.

Six of the figures are on display at Vent Haven Museum and arrived on November 20, 1940.

April 4

Did you know that Jay Johnson was only 10-years-old when he was hired for his first paid job as a ventriloquist? He performed with his earliest figure, a Jerry Mahoney puppet that he named, "Squeaky".

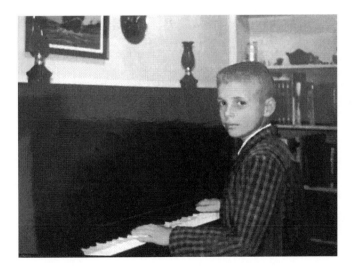

It was for the Spring Lions Club Ladies Night in Abernathy, Texas. For his 10-minute performance, he earned $10.00. Today that would be the equivalent of $550.00 per hour. In those early days for the Lions club, to open the act, Jay played a song or two on the piano.

That figure is on display in the Jay Johnson section of Vent Haven Museum.

Groundbreaking ventriloquist John W. Cooper's intricate and ingenious scenario, "Fun in the Barbershop" involved five separate figures operated at the same time and was extremely popular with audiences of all races. Cooper, portraying the barber, manipulated the figures with wires attached to his feet.

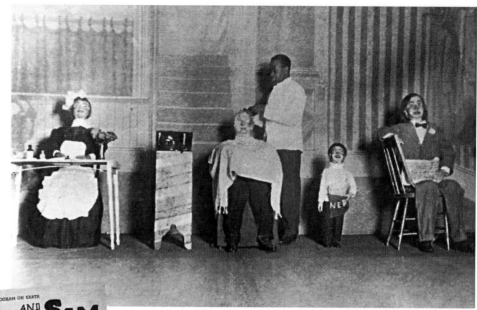

The Daily Nonpareil newspaper of Council Bluffs, Iowa wrote: "…the most talented ventriloquist ever seen."

Later, known as "The Polite Ventriloquist," he was in high demand at all of New York City's social events. He even coached a young Shari Lewis. Cooper continued to perform until he passed away at the age of 93.

April 6

I'm No Dummy, the critically acclaimed comedy documentary, was released on this day in 2010. Director Bryan W. Simon conceived of the project while he was on a bike ride.

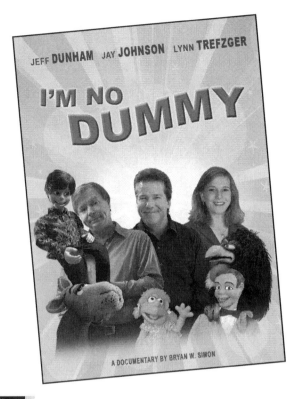

54 ventriloquists and scholars were interviewed for the first feature length documentary about ventriloquism, with 19 appearing in the film. In less than a year, over 150 hours of interview and concert/performance footage was shot. The final film was edited down to 85 minutes in length.

April 7

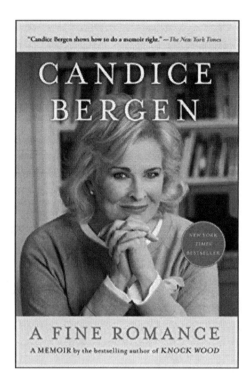

On this day in 2015, Edgar Bergen's daughter, Candice Bergen, published her second memoir, *A Fine Romance*. She points out that Edgar left her nothing, but bequeathed $10,000 to his dummy Charlie McCarthy.

Candice says, "I'd chased my father's approval all my life, and here was proof I'd never get it. I was hurt, shocked, when I discovered he had left me out of his will."

She believed that her father had provided this inheritance for the dummy so that the funds could be managed, invested, and reinvested to provide for his future performances. She said her father wrote in his will: "I make this provision for sentimental reasons, which to me are vital due to the association with Charlie McCarthy, who has been my constant companion and who has taken on the character of a real person and from whom I have never been separated even for a day."

April 8

On this day in 2006, Jeff Dunham's first Comedy Central special premiered. It was called *Jeff Dunham: Arguing with Myself* and was released four days later on DVD. The show was taped in Santa Ana, California. Featured were the characters: Walter, Sweet Daddy D, Peanut, Bubba J, and José Jalapeño on a Stick. Numerous specials and series followed on Comedy Central, Netflix, and broadcast television.

Did you know that the first real figure Willie Tyler had as a boy was a Jerry Mahoney puppet given to him by Madeline Maher of The Maher School of Ventriloquism? His grade school teacher, Thelma Baldwin, drove him to meet Fred and Madeleine Maher. Madeleine painted Jerry Mahoney dark brown and Willie named him J.J.

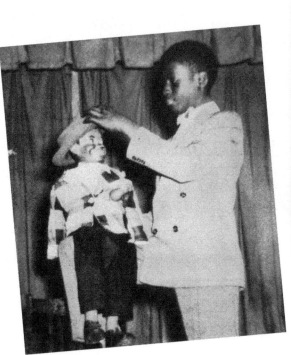

April 10

On this day in 1964, the *Twilight Zone* episode "Caesar and Me" premiered. It was Season 5, Episode 28 and was the second time the TV series featured ventriloquism. Jackie Cooper portrayed ventriloquist Jonathan West.

Puppet maker Revello Petee originally created the dummy in the 40s that was used in this episode. That same figure was used earlier in the *Twilight Zone* episode, "The Dummy."

April 10

On this date in 1963, Señor Wences performed in Danny Kaye's vaudeville Broadway show. The sold-out, limited engagement (47 performances) was staged at the Ziegfeld Theatre located at Sixth Avenue and 54th Street in New York City.

April 11

Today is the birthday of figure maker Austin Phillips, one of a new generation of artisans in the vent community. While there are numerous young makers of soft puppets, few carry on the tradition of creating hard figures. The figures he creates, while uniquely his own, are influenced by the old masters. His new materials and techniques expand the art of figure making.

Many contemporary artists have used ventriloquism to express their ideas; one is Asta Gröting, who works in a variety of media such as sculpture, performance, and video.

For *The Inner Voice* (1993-2015), Gröting explored ventriloquism as a performative instrument to research the soul and its inner workings in a series of videos depicting conversations between a dummy created by the artist and ventriloquists from all over the world. Some of these ventriloquists were Stevo Schüling, Willie Tyler, Ronn Lucas, as well as Buddy Big Mountain, Wendy Morgan, Jennifer Field, Lise Maurais, and Pietro Ghislandi.

April 13

Did you know that innovative figure maker Steve Axtell's mother, Catherine, taught him to use scissors and thread to make his first puppet at age six? Here's a picture of Steve at age 14 from the Sandusky, Ohio newspaper with some of his creations. The clipping was sent to Jim Henson who introduced him to some puppet organizations and encouraged Steve to discover his own unique style. This was an early turning point in Steve's career pursuing a direction for unique character design.

Today, Steve Axtell makes puppets for many of the current ventriloquists and has been doing so for over four decades.

April 14

On this day in 1961, ventriloquist Paul Winchell received US Patent No 3,129,001 for his Inverted Novelty Mask known to kids everywhere as "Ozwald."

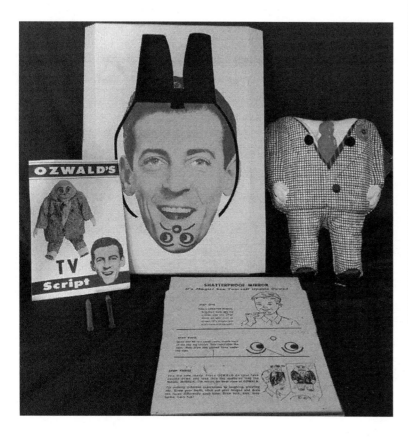

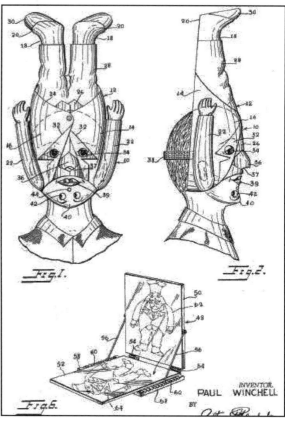

Berwin Novelties introduced a home version of the character that included an Ozwald body, creative pencils to draw the eyes and nose, and a "magic mirror" that automatically turned a reflection upside-down.

After President Kennedy's assassination in 1963, Ozwald's name was changed to Mr. Goody Good.

April 15

Nina Conti's stage show, *Dolly Mixtures*, was recorded at Leeds City Varieties music hall on this day in 2014 and was released on DVD November 24, 2014.

April 16

Did you know that today is Carla Rhodes birthday?

New York Magazine dubbed Carla one of the "Ten New Comedians That Funny People Find Funny." In June of 2018, she performed in Iceland as part of *Reykjavik Cabaret* and taught ventriloquism at the National Museum.

April 17

Today is the birthday of the "surrealist ventriloquist" Señor Wences (April 17, 1896 – April 20, 1999). Born Wenceslao Moreno Centeno in Salamanca, Spain, Señor Wences had the longest career of any ventriloquist, lasting well over seven decades.

Originally wanting to be a professional bullfighter, Wences realized that there was a less dangerous form of entertainment. He was an excellent juggler and for a circus combined that skill with his gift for ventriloquism. That led to nightclub appearances. He would entertain for months at one venue and even had a seven-year stint at the Crazy Horse Saloon in Paris.

April 18

Today is the birthday of Jeff Dunham. No ventriloquist has made more money from the art form than Jeff. He is an *I'm No Dummy* doc alum.

When Dunham was in the sixth grade, he attended the Vent Haven ConVENTion for the first time, and it is here that he met Jimmy Nelson. Jeff Dunham has missed only one ConVENTion.

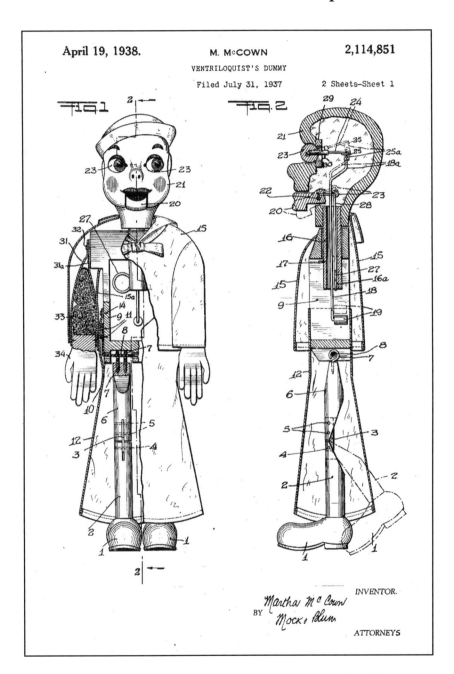

M. McCOWN

VENTRILOQUIST'S DUMMY

Filed July 31, 1937

2,114,851

2 Sheets—Sheet 1

INVENTOR.

Martha McCown

BY *Mock & Blum*

ATTORNEYS

On this date in 1938, Martha McCown received Patent Number 2,114,851 for a ventriloquist's dummy.

The figure had a full body and articulated knees. The mechanism to manipulate the mouth and eyes was much lower than in the traditional dummy. It is not known whether the puppet was ever made.

April 20

Warren Robert Kingery performed as Bob King from the 1930s to the 1960s with his partner Tiny Pine King. Tiny was a small figure carved by Frank Marshall.

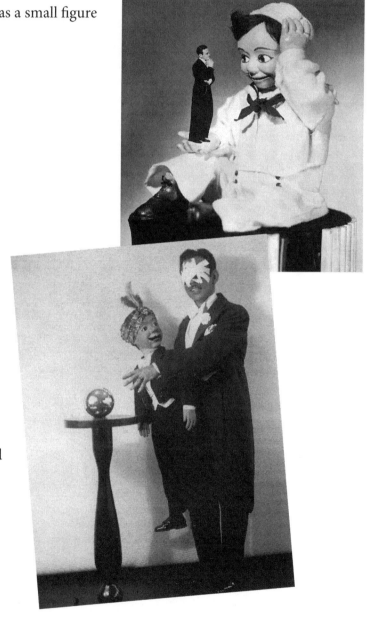

During World War II, King served in the Navy and entertained with Tiny at USO shows, bond rallies, and hospitals. In 1945, King's ship was torpedoed and Tiny sustained some damage as a result of the shockwaves. Tiny Pine King was awarded a medal because of his "injuries." Bob's other main characters were Jewel and Mickey Finn.

April 21

It was in 1945 that Jimmy Nelson asked Chicago figure maker Frank Marshall to construct a new Danny for him. He was still using his "Dummy Dan" figure, which his father modified for better movement, and it was time for a professional figure.

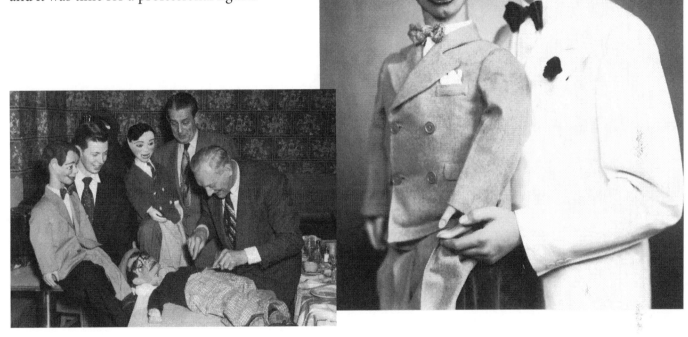

Frank would not carve a partner for anyone unless he could see their act and judge for himself. Jimmy, only 17, was performing weekends at the 1290 seat Englewood Theater at 63rd and Halsted in Chicago. After seeing Jimmy's routine, there was no doubt that Frank would create Danny O'Day and Jimmy performed with that Frank Marshall figure the rest of his career.

April 22

April 27th will be the anniversary of a rather unique ventriloquist event that took place in 2003: "The Ventriloquist Wedding." Ventriloquists Eyvonne Carter and Valentine Vox, along with their puppet partners Twyla and Jeorge, were married at the Imperial Palace Hotel and Casino in Las Vegas during the Las Vegas Ventriloquist Festival with over 200 ventriloquists attending. Not surprisingly, the event attracted press coverage from around the world.

April 23

It was a good week for ventriloquists on television beginning this day in 1951. Between ABC, CBS, NBC, and the Dumont Network, ventriloquists were on eleven times. Max Terhune, Jimmy Nelson, Shirley Dinsdale, Paul Winchell, Edgar Bergen, and Walter Walters are some of the names of those who appeared.

April 24

Buddy Big Mountain became enthralled with ventriloquism after seeing renowned ventriloquist Col. Bill Boley perform at Kaintuck Territory, an old west theme park near Benton, Kentucky.

Buddy and his family did a Native American dance act in the park. Buddy would watch Boley's act day after day and would often be late for his own show. Boley took note of Buddy's dedication and enthusiasm as he took up the art form, mentoring the young performer. A lifelong friendship ensued leading to the career Buddy has today as an international ventriloquial star.

April 25

Figure maker Tim Selberg has made unique figures over the years. For instance, for a Canadian ventriloquist he made a blonde bombshell nude puppet that is anatomically correct, and he crafted a lifelike brain and pop-open skull for Otto Peterson's puppet. He also created Officer von Pork for the CBS series *Broken Badges* used by ventriloquist Jay Johnson.

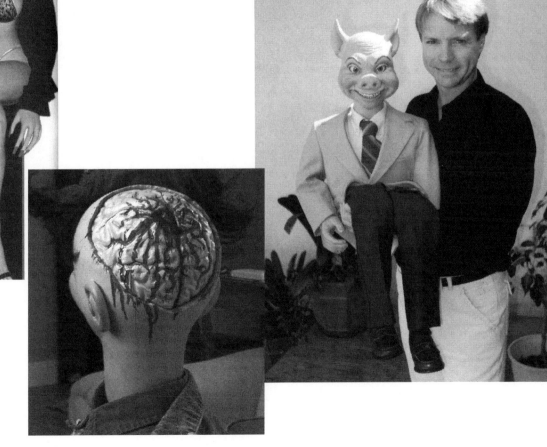

April 26

On this day in 1958, Jimmy Nelson performed publicly for the first time with a new partner, Ftatateeta. It was a television appearance on the *Jimmy Dean Show*.

Nelson said that Ftatateeta was one of his favorite Frank Marshall figures: a beautiful Cheshire cat, colorfully painted and elegantly dressed, with a voice inspired by vaudeville comic Ed Wynn. Her character, a loud-mouthed cat, never really registered with audiences so he retired her. She was also the "spokescat" for a short-lived Nestlé drink called "Keen."

April 27

Today is the birthday of Israeli ventriloquist Allan Blumenstyk. Allan and his partner Jeremiah Jr. have performed with many Israeli jazz musicians as well as with the New Orleans Function Jazz Band. He is also an *I'm No Dummy* alum.

April 28

Taka-Chan arrived from Japan at Vent Haven Museum on this day in 2002. The
partner of Megumi Takahashi, Taka-Chan is one of the more expressive figures
in the museum because her eyebrows can display emotions from anger to
happiness. The design on her kimono is the symbol of the Takahashi family.
Megumi and Taka-Chan presented a gospel-based ventriloquial message, where
puppet Taka-Chan questioned the words and meanings of the lesson.

April 29

On this day in 1951, the *Cincinnati Enquirer* featured W. S. Berger and Vent Haven Museum in their Sunday Pictorial Section.

Antique heads are these found in England. Over 100 years old, they have mouths done in the "nut-cracker" style. Modern dummies have more realistic mouths.

The collector holds aloft a detached head. Ventriloquist can manipulate the various strings to move the dummy's eyes, ears, nose and mouth.

"Champagne Charlie" seems to "walk" with collector Berger. The figure, manipulated by the owner either from the arm or back, can do "the splits."

IRIAL ENQUIRER, Sunday, April 29, 1951.

Three photos of Mr. Berger were prominently featured. One with the life-size Champagne Charlie, one with an Insull head and body, and the third photo was of two antiquarian heads obtained from England. All of these items are still part of Vent Haven Museum today.

137

April 30

Señor Wences was not only an innovative ventriloquist but also a marvelous caricaturist as evidenced by these drawings he did of his act.

When asked for an autograph, Wences would often include a small drawing known as a remarque, of himself or one of his puppet partners.

May 1

Did you know that ventriloquist Jay Johnson was just 15-years-old when he got
a performing job at Six Flags Over Texas? He worked every weekend night show.
The following summer he was hired full time at Six Flags Over Georgia and
performed 917 times, working ten shows a day, seven days a week, with his
partner Squeaky.

This week in 1962, the *Twilight Zone's* "The Dummy" (Season 3, Episode 33) premiered on CBS. Cliff Robertson was ventriloquist Jerry Etherson, and George Murdock played Willie, who transforms into the now human ventriloquist and takes over the act.

In early May 1951, Jimmy Nelson was booked into Minneapolis, Minnesota at the Radisson Hotel's prestigious Flame Room, one of the top nightspots in the city.

Jimmy needed an opening act, so manager Lou Cohan retained a young female singer. Born Elizabeth Mary Mooney, she was given the stage name of "Betty Norman" by her former bandleader George Olsen. The lovely and talented Betty proved to be a hit with the audiences so the duo, along with accompanist Lou Donn, became a touring package for years. After five years together, Jimmy and Betty were married on April 9, 1956.

On this day in 1937, transgender
English ventriloquist Terri Rogers
(May 4, 1937 – May 30, 1999)
was born.

Rogers began life as Ivan Southgate until
the early 1960s when she underwent gender
affirmation surgery. Rogers was a popular
variety act whose career eventually extended
into the 1970s with appearances worldwide,
and notably on HBO's ventriloquist special
"Dummies." An accomplished magician as well,
Rogers was an expert on "topology," the art of
creating illusions with shapes. She wrote three
books on the subject.

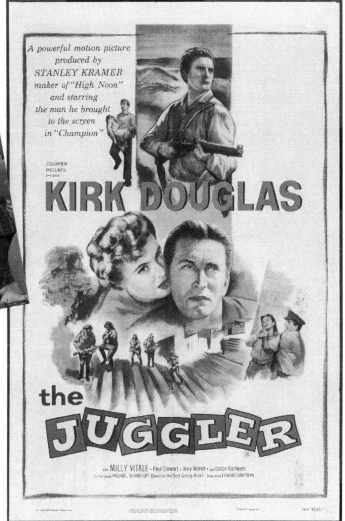

The Juggler was released on this day in 1953. Kirk Douglas portrays famous entertainer Hans Muller, who was imprisoned in the Nazis death camps during World War II. He emigrates to Israel but carries the psychological trauma with him. To comfort a little girl he meets at the camp, Muller performs a simple ventriloquial act a la Señor Wences.

May 6

On this day in 1923, ventriloquist Doris Faye (May 6, 1923 – July 3, 2012) was born.

I can recall when I first saw one of my favorite TV performers, Bozo The Clown, played by a talented and dear man Mr. Bill Britten, at a personal appearance at the Laconia Movie Theater at E. 225 St. and White Plains Rd. in the Bronx.

It was probably 1960 or 1961 and Bozo performed his schitk and engaged the theater audience in songs and games and asked us all to give a loud war whoop for Princess Ticklefeather, the Native American ventriloquist Ms. Doris Faye.

Princess Ticklefeather went up onto the stage where she did comedy skits with her little girl puppet (some sources say her name was "Sunshine", others say her name was "Buttons"). She gave us a lot of ...

had to leave a... George Pal/ MC... Tamblyn, Alan... Sellers, Jessie... Peter Bull, and... and Stan Freb...

The television, Broadway, Las Vegas, and night club performer was best known as Princess Ticklefeather with puppet partner Sunflower. She appeared on the children's shows *Wonderama,* and the *Bozo the Clown Show* airing on WPIX in New York City. Later, Faye returned to more adult entertainment, performing in Las Vegas with an act entitled "The Torso Floor Show." It featured body parts that spoke and had personalities all their own such as the "Talking Top" and "The Living End."

It was on this day in 2009 that the *I'm No Dummy* Facebook page began. It contains 400 videos and photos from the comedy doc and facts about different aspects of ventriloquism. This book was inspired by the Facebook page.

May 8

Vent Haven Museum began as a private collection in the home of W. S. Berger in 1932.

By 1947, Mr. Berger had collected about 100 dummies. With no more room in the house, he renovated his garage and moved the collection there, calling it Vent Haven Annex.

(continued)

By 1963, the collection had outgrown the garage, and Mr. Berger constructed another building that he would eventually name The Josephine Berger Memorial Building. Since Mr. Berger's passing, two other buildings have been used for display. One was built in 1973 and is named the W. S. Berger Memorial Building. The other is a renovated structure called the Jimmy Nelson Building. This building was used by Mr. Berger as a bar. There is a plan for a new museum space.

May 9

Today is the birthday of renowned award-winning Japanese ventriloquist Takeshi Ikeda. He is the founder and chairman of the Japanese Ventriloquist Association and is a mentor, teacher, and inspiration, not only to Japanese ventriloquists, but to ventriloquists all over the world. Takeshi began teaching in 1999 and educates Japanese ventriloquists tirelessly, preparing them for a career in the art form.

Harry (The Great) Lester and side-kick George Byron, Jr., teach ventriloquial tricks to actress Joanne Arnold in Lester's Hollywood studio.

William Shakespeare Berger entertains youngsters at his Fort Mitchell, Kentucky, home, Vent Haven—the unofficial ventriloquism capital of the world.

Secrets of the Talking Dummies

By RUFUS JARMAN

Did you ever hear the story of the dummy that choked when his master drank straight whisky? Of Edgar Bergen's odd will, which leaves $10,000 to Charlie McCarthy? Or of the manikin who couldn't remember his lines? Do some voice throwers *really* think they are two persons? The evidence will surprise you . . .

VENTRILOQUISM—one of the most ancient techniques for fooling the gullible—has been used to evoke pronouncements from the lips of graven images and has been mistaken for the screaming of devils from the bellies of "possessed" people. In the early days of civilization, ventriloquy was regarded as a supernatural manifestation, something to be feared. Today, ventriloquism is a fairly common household word and its practitioners are usually regarded as pretty funny fellows.

Yet, it was only a scant half-dozen years ago that this strange craft faced one of the most important crossroads in its history. The issue was: would it continue as a little-known, mysterious practice, with a relatively small following in theaters, cabarets and side shows, or could it successfully adapt itself to the requirements of television and thus advance into an era of the greatest appeal and popularity in its history?

With the exception of Edgar Bergen and Charlie McCarthy, who are invisible to radio audiences and therefore not essentially a ventriloquial act, few ventriloquists had ever established wide followings, and the chances that any of them would did not look too promising, at first. Paul Winchell, a dark-haired, fairly handsome, completely ambitious young man

from Brooklyn, in association with Jerry Mahoney, a pert-faced wooden figure with a slicked-down red wig, was making a nice wage at the time as a theatrical and night-club entertainer. But even then Winchell had his eyes set on television. A New York advertising agency suggested that he and the eminent "mentalist," Joe Dunninger, combine acts in a movie short that would be shown to prospective sponsors of television shows. Winchell and Dunninger agreed with alacrity, and the film was made.

When no potential sponsors were heard from after several weeks, Winchell's manager telephoned the agency people. They said they were sorry, but apparently television was no medium for ventriloquism, since the voice of Jerry, the dummy, was inaudible on the sound track. Winchell suggested another try, but the agency said no. The movie had cost $6000, and there was nothing mechanically wrong with it.

About that time, Ed Sullivan, the Broadway newspaper columnist, invited Winchell to appear on the opening program of his television variety show, Toast of The Town, on CBS. During rehearsal, Sullivan, from the control room, interrupted Winchell's act to say he couldn't hear the dummy. Winchell increased his ventriloquial voice until he was fit to split a vocal cord, but the control room still

couldn't hear Jerry. Winchell concluded there must be something about a ventriloquial voice that didn't register over a TV microphone. Then he glanced up at the microphone on the boom above him and the mystery was solved.

"Hey!" Winchell yelled at the boom man. "When Jerry is talking, where are you keeping that mike?"

"In front of the dummy's mouth, of course," the man replied.

"So that's been it," Winchell said. "Look, the dummy just seems to be talking. I'm really doing the talking, you see? Keep the mike in front of me all the time."

The boom man did, and Jerry's voice came over fine. Of course, the same thing had happened when the movie was made. Since TV-boom microphones are directional, they pick up only sounds made directly into them, and since sounds never emerge from dummies, the microphone in front of Jerry Mahoney had registered nothing.

Winchell went ahead to become TV's first great ventriloquial star. He makes a quarter of a million dollars a year now, and has a long-term contract with NBC to do a weekly program. He and other television ventriloquists, on view almost daily, have transformed their art from a curiosity to something

24

On this day in 1953, *The Saturday Evening Post* published an article by Rufus Jarman entitled, "Secrets of the Talking Dummies." Those six pages on the history of ventriloquism and W. S. Berger's Vent Haven Museum were read by over 7 million people around the country.

May 10

The Great Lester was known for having created many innovative bits that ventriloquists still use today. Lester originated the three-way telephone conversation, a variation on the "distant voice" routine. He's also credited with being the first to smoke while doing ventriloquism, drinking while doing ventriloquism, and even having a dummy yodel.

150

May 11

On this day in 2009, the *Two and a Half Men*
episode, "Good Morning, Mrs. Butterworth" (Season
6, Episode 23) premiered. Alan Harper (John Cryer)
uses a Goldberger Danny O'Day figure to learn
ventriloquism, causing friction between him and
his older brother Charlie, played by Charlie Sheen.
Danny O'Day appeared several more times
on the series.

May 12

Today is the birthday of British figure maker Edwin Simms (May 12, 1883 - October 1, 1962). Known professionally as A. Quisto, he brought many innovations to the art form.

Quisto claimed to be the first one to use soft and thin lamb or goat skin for the lip and mouth movement mechanism. He also used artificial eyeballs instead of painted eyes, and wigs made of real hair instead of crepe or wool. He made a crawling figure that could go across stage while the vent was occupied with a different dummy. One version used a clockwork motor to move the dummy. In his 30 year career, it is approximated he made 3,000 hard figures. Two of Quisto's clients were British ventriloquists Arthur Prince and Tom Coram. Vent Haven Museum has 13 Quisto figures.

May 13

Vent Haven Museum founder William Shakespeare Berger (May 13, 1878 – June 24, 1972) has a birthday today. W. S., as he was known, purchased his first figure, Tommy Baloney, in 1910 on a trip to New York City, but it was in 1932 when he started his collection in earnest. W. S.'s father was a German Shakespearian actor, hence W. S.'s name.

Did you know that today is International Ventriloquism Day?
The celebratory slogan is "The day speaks for itself."

According to many scholars, ventriloquism is a part of all art forms.
Every piece of art speaks for itself.

What speaks for you?

May 14

Yesterday in 1992, Rosita, one of Vent Haven Museum's most interesting and colorful figures, arrived.

Made, used, and donated by ventriloquist Bill Hume, Rosita was quickly made in three weeks while he was stationed overseas in 1943. The USO was looking for performers and Hume did not have time to send for his other figures, so he carved Rosita out of light balsa wood, and, to avoid mechanical failure in the jungles, the mouth was operated by a lever and closed by a lead weight. Rosita and Hume retired in 1953 after years of touring for the USO.

May 15

On this day in 1950, *Time* magazine featured a picture of Podine Puffington, Edgar Bergen's five-foot-tall female puppet. She first appeared in Bergen's show at The Desert Inn in Las Vegas and subsequently was seen on some of his television appearances. *Life* magazine also featured pictures of Podine.

No. 12 J. M. DUMMY
Suggested retail: $14.98

No. 20 J. M. MOVING EYES
Suggested retail: $24.98

No. 24 J. M. VENTRO DOLL
Suggested retail: $6.98

No. 36 K
Suggeste

JURO NOVELTY CO., Inc., 18 East 18th Street, New York 3, New York
Manufacturers of JURO Celebrity Dolls.

How to be a
Ventriloquist
By
PAUL
WINCHELL

Assisted by
JERRY MAHONEY

INCLUDING A BIOGRAPHY OF PAUL WINCHELL
AND A HISTORY OF VENTRILOQUISM

During the run of *The Paul Winchell and Jerry Mahoney Show* on NBC, Paul Winchell received 18,000 fan letters a week, several hundreds from children seeking ventriloquial advice. In 1949, Winchell and the Juro Novelty Company teamed up to make an inexpensive Jerry Mahoney vent puppet. It came with a how-to-book on ventriloquism written by Winchell. Up until that time, Juro made only dolls, but, by 1953 Juro sold over a half a million of these toy dummies.

On this day in 1900, *The Wonderful Wizard of Oz* was published. Written by L. Frank Baum and illustrated by W. W. Denslow, the book featured "The Wizard" who was known as a skilled ventriloquist working for Bailum & Barney's Great Consolidated Shows. He was able to imitate any bird, beast, or human (male or female). Oz would explain to Dorothy and her friends that these illusions were made possible by dummies and other special effect props.

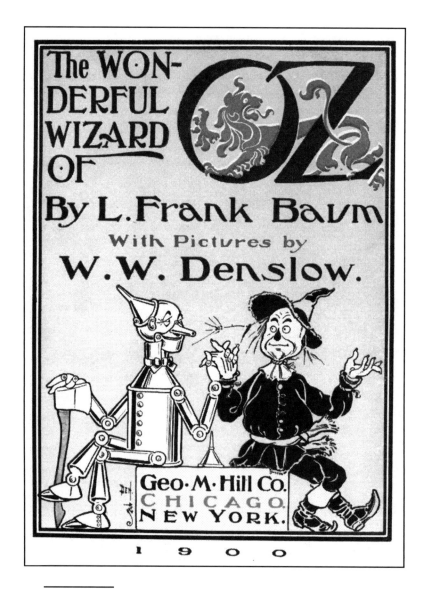

Jay Johnson was just six years old when he first saw Big Jon and Sparky at Lubbock Texas Civic Center. This revelation of a talking puppet come to life was the impetus for his lifelong career in ventriloquism. Big Jon and his puppet partner, Sparky, had a morning children's radio show entitled *No School Today*. Jay listened religiously to the show and when his parents took him to see his heroes live, he learned that Big Jon did the voice of Sparky.

Happy Birthday to Vonda Kay Van Dyke. Vonda was crowned Miss America 1965 at the 38th *Miss America Pageant*, on September 12, 1964. It was held at the Boardwalk Hall in Atlantic City, New Jersey and broadcast on the CBS Network. She is an *I'm No Dummy* alum.

Vonda was the first contestant to use ventriloquism in the talent competition. She and her partner Kurly Q were nearly rejected from the pageant because the rules specified contestants only perform solo. The judges figured out that her partner was a dummy and the two were allowed to perform.

On this day in 2000, Shari Lewis won her 12th Emmy® Award. It was bestowed posthumously as she had passed on August 2, 1998, at the age of 65. The award for Outstanding Performer in a Children's Series was for *The Charlie Horse Music Pizza* show.

May 20

On this day in 2006, eleven of Chris Cross' (October 30, 1907 – October 7, 1989) figures arrived at the Vent Haven Museum including Looie, Baby Doll, and Syracuse.

CREDITS: TIVOLI CIRCUIT - AUSTRALIA
RADIO CITY MUSIC HALL - N.Y. - RETURN
MOULIN ROUGE - PARIS - 4TH RETURN
PALADIUM - LONDON - RECORD RUN
SAVOY HOTEL - LONDON - HELD OVER
COMMAND PERFORMANCE
CASA du LIBON - LEBANON
SAHARA - LAS VEGAS

INTERNATIONAL ENTERTAINER
CHRIS CROSS
COMEDY WITH A PLUS

The most fascinating of the eleven figures was the life-size Christine. Chris built and performed with Christine in the 1940s and 1950s. She was banned from American television because of her pivoting bosom. Christine was originally named Goldie.

When ventriloquist Señor Wences first came to America in 1935, he would often face suspicious and even hostile nightclub audiences who thought he had a recording device under his table when he was performing with Johnny. He traveled with a tall table to show that nothing was concealed. He even quit smoking on stage because audiences thought there was a recording device in the cigarette.

On May 13, 1993 the characters, Arthur Crandall and Gabbo, appeared for the first time on the *The Simpsons* in an episode entitled "Krusty Gets Kancelled" (Season 4, Episode 22).

When they get to Springfield, Crandall and Gabbo have a children's TV show that airs opposite Krusty the Clown. They are so successful, in fact, that they force Krusty into cancellation.

Gabbo's catchphrase was "I'm a bad widdle boy!" and the figure gets his name from the title character of the 1929 film *The Great Gabbo*. Arthur Crandall and Gabbo, both voiced by Hank Azaria, appeared four more times on the show, in *The Simpson's Movie*, and in the Simpson's video game.

May 23

Tomorrow marks the anniversary of the world premiere of *I'm No Dummy* at the Seattle International Film Festival in 2009. The documentary, a huge hit at the festival, sold out an unheard of three shows. The question and answer session, starring Jay Johnson and Bob, Lynn Trefzger and Chloe, and Tom Ladshaw and Thelonius, along with producer Marjorie Engesser and director Bryan W. Simon, followed the first two screenings and was the talk of the festival.

May 23

On this day in 1954, life-size walking figure Jonathan Jones arrived at Vent Haven Museum. Used by Swedish ventriloquist Finn Borjesson, Jonathan was made by Len Insull.

En öm scen på Lv 2:s revy i Linköping mellan "sergeant" Dickey Doll och Gun-Britt Jonsson, bevittnades med intresse av magikern mr Carboni, t. v., revypappan Finn Börjesson och Lisbeth Hjalmarsson.

Jonathan has a dizzying array of features including winking, blinking, moving eyes, moving eyebrows, and smiling. He can smoke, walk, and has a remote control to make him smile without the ventriloquist being next to him. Jonathan Jones is featured in *I'm No Dummy 2* and appears in photographer Matthew Rolston's book *Talking Heads: The Vent Haven Portraits*.

May 24

On this day in 1958, Jimmy Nelson and his partners performed for President Eisenhower and the Washington Press Corps at the 32nd Annual Dinner for the White House Correspondents Association (WHCA). After the gala, Jimmy and his wife Betty sat with Vice President Richard Nixon. The Vice President wanted a picture with Danny and Farfel but couldn't get one, exclaiming, "All this press and no one has a camera?"

Thirty-second

Annual Dinner

of the

White House

Correspondents' Association

★ ★

Hotel Statler
Saturday, May 24, 1958
Washington, D. C.

THE WHITE HOUSE
CORRESPONDENTS' ASSOCIATION
proudly presents
"THINGS ARE BETTER THAN EVER"
A TIMELY SALUTE TO THE COST OF LIVING

(NOTE: *As it must to all organizations, the recession has hit us, too. To save money on the orchestra, we have placed at each table a supply of combs and thin paper. Fold the paper about the comb and hum any tune you desire. Remember, President Eisenhower says you can't expect the government to do everything.*)

JINX FALKENBURG AND THE CANDLEWICK PLAYERS
JIMMY NELSON AND COMPANY
JOE MAIZE AND HIS SONS OF PLENTY
PEGGY KING
MIKE NICHOLS AND ELAINE MAY
AND
VAN CLIBURN

THE ENTIRE PERFORMANCE MAY BE BLAMED ON OUR PRODUCER,
JOEL MARGOLIS OF THE CAPITOL THEATER

DINNER MUSIC BY THE UNITED STATES NAVY BAND
UNDER THE DIRECTION OF
COMMANDER CHARLES BRENDLER

SHOW MUSIC BY EDDIE PIERCE AND THE
LOCAL 814 SYMPHONETTE

As usual, we are indebted to a host of generous friends for our show tonight. Without them, this might have been possible, but what an awful thought.
Our deepest thanks to Harry Kalcheim of the William Morris Agency, Orville Crouch of Loew's Inc., Earl Wilson of the *New York Post*, James C. Petrillo, President of the American Federation of Musicians, Jackie Bright of the American Guild of Variety Artists, Beverly Roberts of Theater Authority, Harold Hoffman of the Screen Actors Guild, and William Judd of Columbia Artists Management, Inc.
Piano by Steinway. Lighting by PEPCO.
Transportation for our artists tonight was furnished by Regal Shoes.

In 1961, Jimmy Nelson was asked to host his own New York City area show. It was called *Studio 99 1/2* and was taped live Monday through Friday at 5:30 PM, with a repeat airing at 9:30 AM the following day. The half-hour show was designed for children but also appealed to adults. Jimmy would often perform twelve or thirteen different voices with as many characters throughout a single episode of the show.

On this day in 1993, ventriloquists Shari Lewis and Mallory Lewis became
the first mother/daughter writing team to win an Emmy® Award. They
won Outstanding Writing in a Children Series for *Lamb Chop's Play-Along*.
Shari also won one of her twelve Emmys® that day for Outstanding Performer
in a Children's Series. The show ran on PBS for four seasons from
January 13, 1992 to September 22, 1995.

May 27

Today is British ventriloquist Saveen's birthday (May 27, 1914 – April 14, 1994). Born Albert Edward Langford, in the late 40s and 50s he was the only professional male ventriloquist with a female puppet as his main partner.

Saveen had been injured by a 500-pound exploding bomb during World War II and suffered nearly fatal damage to his lungs. According to Saveen, his recuperation exercises involved breathing with just one lung at a time, and it was through this method, that he was able to develop the tiny voice of his main character, the extremely popular Daisy May.

Saveen with the Colonel, Andy Lang, the Dog and Daisy May.   He has ten voices, uses seven of them

Yesterday in 1950, *Ventriloquist Cat,* a seven-minute MGM animated film directed by Tex Avery was released.

After a cat is caught graffitiing "I hate Dogs," Spike, a dim-witted bulldog chases him. The cat finds a gadget similar to the "Ventrilo" that helps him throw his voice and tricks the gullible canine into looking for him in a variety of dangerous spots. *Ventriloquist Cat* was later remade in CinemaScope as *Cat's Meow,* released in 1957.

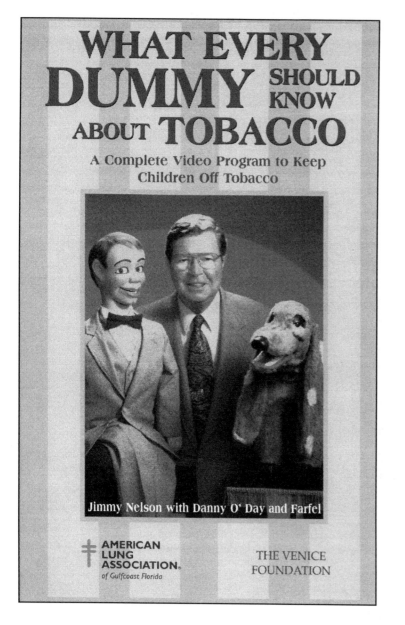

In 2000, Jimmy Nelson produced an educational video, *What Every Dummy Should Know About Tobacco.*

This entertaining program was presented in elementary schools. In the video Jimmy "taught" Danny O'Day the dangers of smoking, but it was the school children who learned valuable lessons. Jimmy had often performed his signature "smoking bit" with Danny, but, after doing this video, he retired that part of his act.

May 30

On this day in 1911, ventriloquist Clifford Guest (May 30, 1911 - July 15, 2002) was born. Clifford Guest was not only a traditional ventriloquist but also an acoustic illusionist or polyphonist.

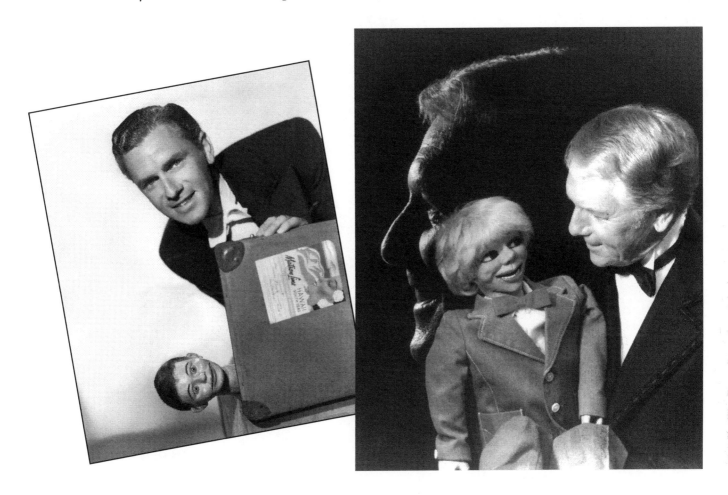

Ventriloquists used polyphony before they utilized figures and Guest continued that tradition with great success. Billed as a "Ventro-Impressionist," one of his famed vocal illusions permitted the audience to hear a military parade complete with aircraft, shooting artillery, commands, and marching.

It's traditional that when a ventriloquist retires or dies, the puppet partner retires as well. However, Lamb Chop continues to perform with Shari Lewis' daughter, Mallory Lewis. Mallory, an *I'm No Dummy* alum, has performed all over the world with Lamb Chop and now has a musical tribute stage show entitled *A Shari Lewis Legacy*.

June 1

Doing ventriloquism is without a doubt acting, and talented ventriloquists have shown their acting chops in another way by performing without their puppet partners.

 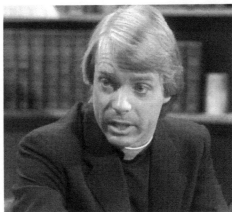

Shari Lewis guest starred on various television shows like *The Man From Uncle*. Jay Johnson appeared in stage plays and many times on television; on the show *Gimme A Break!* he played a priest. Paul Winchell had a recurring role as Dr. Putnum on *The Lucy Show,* and Edgar Bergen portrayed Grandpa Zebb Walton in the film *The Homecoming: A Christmas Story*. Bergen was offered the opportunity to reprise his role on *The Waltons* TV series but passed because of the arduous shooting schedule.

June 2

Today is soft puppet figure maker Melissa Taylor's birthday. Melissa joined her mother Mary Ann at MAT Puppets in 2005, giving up a career in law, to become one of the preeminent soft figure makers in the world.

The two have produced amazing puppets over the years and ventriloquists worldwide are grateful Melissa made the career change.

June 3

On this date in 1950, Paul Winchell and Jerry Mahoney guest-starred on the TV variety show, *Cavalcade of Stars*. Illustrating the extent of Paul's imagination, he wrote a sketch in which Jerry dreams he switches places with Paul, who becomes the "dummy." Jerry exacts his revenge on Paul by smashing his face into a cream pie. The sketch is funny, unique, and deeply psychological.

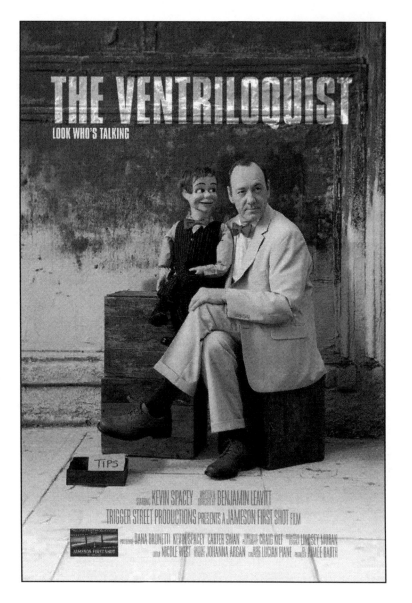

In June 2012, an eleven-minute short film entitled *The Ventriloquist* premiered in New York City. It stars Academy® Award-winning actor Kevin Spacey as Frank, a ventriloquist who has occupied the same corner for the past three years. His partner, Mr. Higgins, is Frank's more outgoing and angrier alter ego. When Mr. Higgins goes missing, Frank finds his own voice.

June 5

Happy Birthday to British ventriloquist Nina Conti.

Nina is a groundbreaking and imaginative ventriloquist who won the British Comedy award in 2013. She's also an internet sensation, star of BBC's *Live at the Apollo*, and Russell Howard's *Good News*.

Charlie McCarthy was not always the character that we have come to know. Early in Edgar Bergen's career, Charlie was an Irish newspaper boy. When Bergen realized that vaudeville was dying, and that night clubs and supper clubs were the next entertainment venues, he decided to change the act's appearance and material.

The sophisticated Charlie McCarthy made his debut at the Helen Morgan Club in New York City in 1936. Dressed identically in white ties, tops hats, and tails, the duo was a huge success and began to tour the top vaudeville theaters in the United States.

June 7

Bob Evans' (August 23, 1915 - October 18, 1951) only partner Jerry O'Leary resides at Vent Haven Museum and was donated in 1976 by Virginia Grand, his widow. Bob paid just $3.98 for Jerry who was originally a Willie Talk doll that he then modified. He began using the figure in 1937, working constantly. The two appeared together in the 1944 musical comedy film *Hey Rookie*. Evans also influenced the art form by mentoring ventriloquist Jimmy Nelson. Bob was only 36-years-old when he died tragically in a car accident.

June 8

Many people believe that Señor Wences made his American television debut on the *The Ed Sullivan Show*. Actually, it was this day in 1948 on the first episode of *Milton Berle's Texaco Star Theater*.

June 9

Tomorrow, June 10th, is the birthday of Terry Fator. Terry appeared in the extras of *I'm No Dummy* and then in *I'm No Dummy 2*. Terry has had one of the hottest shows in Vegas for over 10 years at his own theater in The Mirage resort and casino.

June 10

On this date in 2007, Jay Johnson won the Tony® Award for "Best Special Theatrical Event" for *Jay Johnson: The Two and Only!*

Although several ventriloquists, including Ricky Layne, Señor Wences, Ronn Lucas, and Jeff Dunham, have appeared on Broadway, Johnson is the first and only ventriloquist to have his own show and win an American Theatre Wing Tony® Award as well as a Los Angeles Ovation Award.

June 11

The Vent Haven Museum got its first official logo in 2011.
It was designed by Jeff Dionise.

June 12

This week in 2014, acclaimed photographer Matthew Rolston had an exhibition entitled "Talking Heads" at the Diane Rosenstein Fine Art Gallery in Los Angeles. It consisted of monumental color portraits measuring sixty inches square, depicting dummies chosen from a collection of ventriloquists' figures housed at Vent Haven Museum.

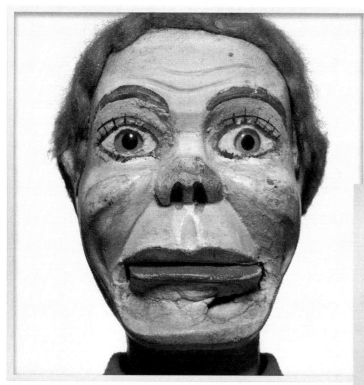

I'm No Dummy director Bryan W. Simon and producer Marjorie Engesser represented Vent Haven Museum at the opening night reception.

June 13

Did you know that Col. Bill Boley's (September 9, 1935 – December 17, 2000) partner Freddy was kidnapped? As the story goes, someone stole Freddy in his case out of Bill Boley's car and left a ransom note. Boley publicized the kidnapping and the wire services picked it up, reaching papers across the country. All the publicity caused the kidnappers to lose their nerve. They tossed the case out of their car and bystanders found Freddy inside.

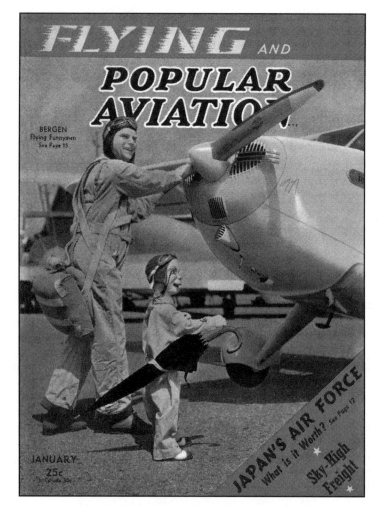

Edgar Bergen was so enthralled with flying that he owned three aircraft as well as the Montebello Airport, which he purchased in 1947. He was an excellent pilot. Charlie McCarthy, his wooden partner, also loved to fly as evidenced by the fact Charlie had his own membership in the Aircraft Owners and Pilots Association (AOPA). His number was APOA 31800-A, and the two of them, along with Mortimer Snerd and Effie Klinker, often flew together to their performances.

(continued)

June 15

Edgar Bergen and Jeff Dunham are both pilots who have been highlighted in aeronautic magazines. Dunham was featured in the June/July 2012 issue of *Heli Pilot* magazine as he flies model helis and personal helis. Edgar Bergen was featured in *Flying and Popular Aviation* magazine in January 1941. Jeff is such an enthusiast he acknowledged in *I'm No Dummy,* if he were not a ventriloquist, he'd most likely be a full-time helicopter pilot.

June 16

On this day in 1939, Grace Larsen, known as Madam Pinxy, organized the first successful meeting of ventriloquists.

It took place at the International Brotherhood of Magicians (IBM) convention in Battle Creek, Michigan. She believed that ventriloquists should have their own organization and is credited as the organizer/founder of the International Brotherhood of Ventriloquists (IBV). *(continued)*

Madam Pinxy got the ball rolling by having a "Jam Session" where 60 ventriloquists got together to share ideas and information and perform for one another. In 1940, a year after that first "Jam Session," the idea of the IBV was officially recognized and temporary officers were elected with support and blessing of the IBM. In June 1941 the IBV was officially formed in Cincinnati, Ohio for amateur and professional ventriloquists. Yearly dues were $1.00.

June 18

Yesterday on June 17, 1921, ventriloquist Peter Badrich (June 17, 1921 – August 13, 2015) was born. Known by the stage name Peter Rich, he did not like working with a microphone and avoided it as much as possible. Rich believed that the illusion was superior without it.

He had three primary puppet partners: Oscar Westin, Rawhide, and Zingo. Zingo was most unusual and all were made by Frank Marshall. Rich not only performed on the traditional stages and the television shows of the time but was also a spokesperson for Westinghouse from the 1950s through the 1960s, appearing at appliance and department stores and houseware fairs.

June 19

In 1950 Wichita, Kansas, during the third and last very late night show, Jimmy Nelson's iconic dog partner Farfel was born.

Jimmy picked up a stuffed dog left behind by a patron and started improvising with it. He knew he had something; as a result, his second most famous character emerged. Lou Donn, Jimmy's musical accompanist, had a habit of calling everyone he met "Farfel," which Jimmy thought was funny. After Frank Marshall built the dog, Jimmy named his new partner Farfel.

June 20

It isn't certain if legendary figure maker Frank Marshall invented the ball and socket configuration for the neck and body, but one thing is certain: he popularized and advanced this extremely simple yet innovative way to make the figure work more smoothly. Not only was it easier to manipulate than the flat neck, but also the figure could perform in a more lifelike fashion by allowing the head to swivel and nod in a much more realistic way.

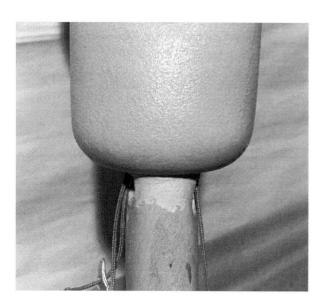

June 21

Vent Haven Museum has approximately 250,000 pieces of correspondence in their archives and library. W. S. Berger kept every letter he received and also a carbon of every letter he sent out. Many of these letters are from modern ventriloquists who corresponded with W. S. when they were young, as well as great ventriloquists from the distant past.

June 22

Did you know that today is the birthday of Stanley Burns (June 22, 1919 – July 29, 1998)?

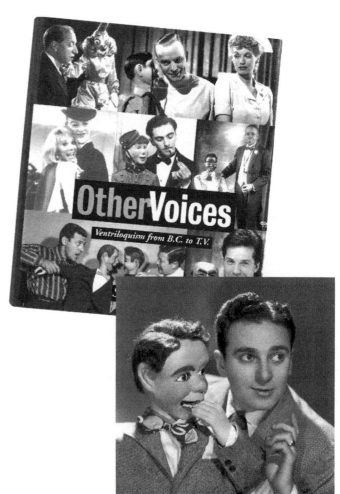

Stanley wrote the book *Other Voices: Ventriloquism from B.C. to TV* and was the first ventriloquist to develop a radio controlled, remotely operated ventriloquial figure.

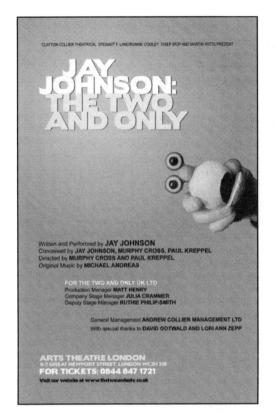

On this date in 2008, the European premiere of *Jay Johnson: The Two And Only!* opened at the Arts Theater on London's West End. *The London Free Press* praised the show: "…ecstatic applause from delighted audiences for a performance like no other currently running on a West End stage."

Did you know that in 1905 when
The Great Lester was headlining on
vaudeville stages around the world,
he was making an unheard of sum of
$3000.00 dollars per week? That's
the equivalent of $86,000.00 a week
today. Unfortunately, he did not
handle his money well and was pen-
niless by the end of vaudeville
in the 1930s.

June 25

On this day in 2016, curator Lisa Sweasy's book about Vent Haven Museum was published. It features a history of the museum and its founder, W. S. Berger, along with information on some of the most interesting figures and a "How To" guide" by Tom Ladshaw on the practice of ventriloquism.

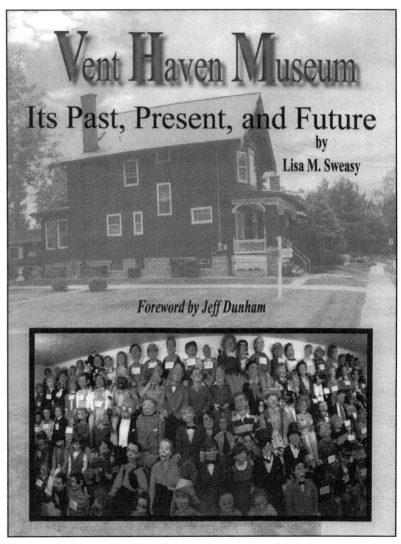

June 26

Roy Douglas was known as "The Singing Ventriloquist" with his partner Eddie Echo and received great reviews wherever he performed.

He also performed with a conjoined twins figure called, "Pip and Flip" made by John Carroll. Douglas was also known as a figure maker, which he wasn't. The figures he sold through his catalog were actually made by John Carroll. To help carry out the ruse, there's an "open letter" from John Carroll in the Roy Douglas catalogue in which Carroll states that he himself owns a "Douglas dummy."

June 27

Ed Sullivan and his 23 years of variety shows made an indelible impact on the art of ventriloquism, bringing the art week after week into homes across the country. It was on this day in 1948 that a ventriloquist act was featured by Ed Sullivan on the first *Toast of the Town*. That ventriloquist was Paul Winchell, and he and Jerry Mahoney helped usher in a new era of ventriloquism on television.

June 28

It was on this day in 1946 that the British film *Dead of Night* premiered in the United States.

The Ealing Studios film was a five-part anthology of stories and in "The Ventriloquist's Dummy," Maxwell Frere, played by Michael Redgrave, is a ventriloquist who believes his partner is actually alive. British ventriloquist Arthur Brough's dummy "Tim" was used in this film. In *I'm No Dummy 2*, Jay Johnson elucidates why ventriloquists are often portrayed this way on film and TV.

June 29

Ventriloquial figures and ventriloquists have helped promote countless products on television, radio and in print throughout the years. Shari Lewis and Lamb Chop promoted hotdogs. Señor Wences hawked fountain pens. And Edgar Bergen and Charlie McCarthy promoted products from Coca Cola to GE lightbulbs and even cheese for Kraft.

(continued)

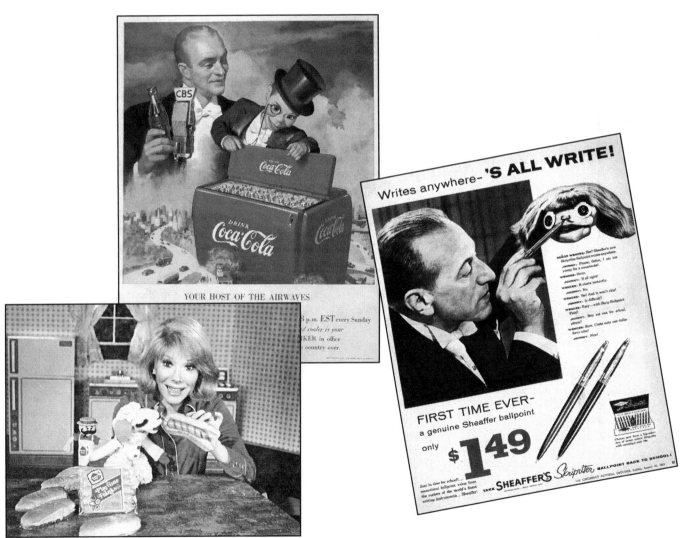

June 30

Paul Winchell and Jerry Mahoney recommended Emerson televisions and dress shirts. Jay Johnson was asked to design a figure and sponsor Frogurt for a national campaign. The puppet's name was Farmer Frogurt. And the very famous Nestlé's products were promoted by Jimmy Nelson.

One of the more unusual campaigns was in the late 1980s for safe sex entitled "Even dummies wear condoms," featuring a classic Frank Marshall figure.

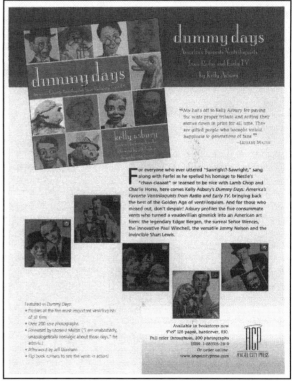

On this day in 2003, Kelly Asbury's book, *Dummy Days*, about the golden age of ventriloquism was published. It profiles five performers who turned a vaudevillian gimmick into an American art form: Edgar Bergen, Paul Winchell, Jimmy Nelson, Señor Wences and Shari Lewis.

July 2

Paul Winchell was awarded 17.8 million dollars on this day in 1986 from his lawsuit against KTTV and Metromedia. They threatened to erase all episodes of his *Winchell-Mahoney Time* television program that ran from 1965 through 1968.

They thought Winchell would sign a new contract to save the tapes and when he didn't, they destroyed the tapes. Metromedia appealed all the way to the U.S. Supreme Court but the case was rejected. Even though Paul won, all of those great shows are now lost forever. Of the 305 episodes that Winchell taped, only 17 survived.

July 3

Creative and innovative British ventriloquist Phil D'Rey (July 3, 1898 – June 19, 1970) was born today in 1898.

Born David Cuthbert, he performed internationally for many decades. When D'Rey first came to America, he entertained throughout the southern states in tent and medicine shows, and then appeared on screen in silent films with Charlie Chaplin, Lon Chaney, and Victor McLaglen. Often booked for long runs of four shows a night, he played for six months at the Bismarck Hotel in Chicago and eight months as the featured act with the *International Parade* in Cairo, Egypt.

July 4

Today is the birthday of Louis Albert Brandetta, who uses the stage names Russo Lewis and Russ Lewis. An extreme comedic rapid-fire exchange was Lewis' specialty with his puppet partner New Yorker "Brooklyn Birch."

For a short period of time, he had his own children's show on KTTV in Los Angeles. One critic commented "His facile vocal changes are so quick and natural that it sometimes seems that the dummy is doing the venting."

Did you know that the first section director Bryan W. Simon completed for the *I'm No Dummy* documentary was the Señor Wences section?

Señor Wences is one of Simon's favorite ventriloquists and that segment was developed early to show reluctant interviewees what the film would be like. It was never changed or reedited. The film went from concept to completion in just one year.

It was in 1978 that the Village of Decatur, Michigan named a street for their favorite son, Edgar Bergen. The approximately 1.13 mile Edgar Bergen Boulevard is on the north side of the village. The city also renamed a school Edgar Bergen Elementary in his honor. Bergen lived on a farm near Decatur until he was four-years-old, and is one of only two ventriloquists to have a street named after him. Do you remember who the other is? (See January 2 for the answer.)

July 7

This month in 1983, a show hosted by a ventriloquist became the first straight-to-video children's program. Channel Video of Winchester, England released *My Video Party*. The show was hosted by ventriloquist Valentine Vox with his puppet partner Jeorge and was videotaped by Lacewing Productions.

July 8

Final rehearsals began for *Il Tiempo Postino* (*Postman Time*) this week in 2007. The show premiered on July 12, 2007 at the Manchester Opera House in Manchester, England.

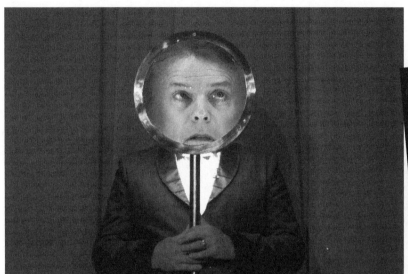

Starring ventriloquist Jay Johnson, and other talented individuals in various artistic disciplines, this unusual stage presentation was a group exhibition that occupied time rather than space. The performance was presented again in June of 2009 in Basil, Switzerland.

July 9

Today is puppet maker Smith Handerson's birthday. He is a creative and talented hand and glove puppet maker. Smith's puppets have been described as "vibrant, cartoony, abstract, and even surreal at times." No two puppets are alike; each is a unique work of fun puppetry art.

He creates well over 200 unique puppets every year with each one taking approximately a day and a half. He'll gather up a bunch of parts, and keep rearranging them until he comes up with a new face for his latest creation.

July 10

German ventriloquist Erich Mast, who went by the stage name Erich Everty (July 10, 1902 – January 12, 1958), was born on this day according to Everty's application to the International Brotherhood of Ventriloquists. His German obituary, however, stated he was born in 1907.

His main partners were Ruland, a chimney sweep, and Felix. Everty would close his act with his partner's legs outside the case. The puppet would exclaim, "Die box ist zu klein" or "The box is too small." Everty would then try to stuff the puppet in, after which an arm or hand would flop out as the puppet continued to scream, "Die box ist zu klein!"

July 11

Happy Birthday to Jay Johnson. This Tony® Award winning ventriloquist is one of the finest ever. As a young ventriloquist, he wrote letters to W. S. Berger asking for advice and guidance.

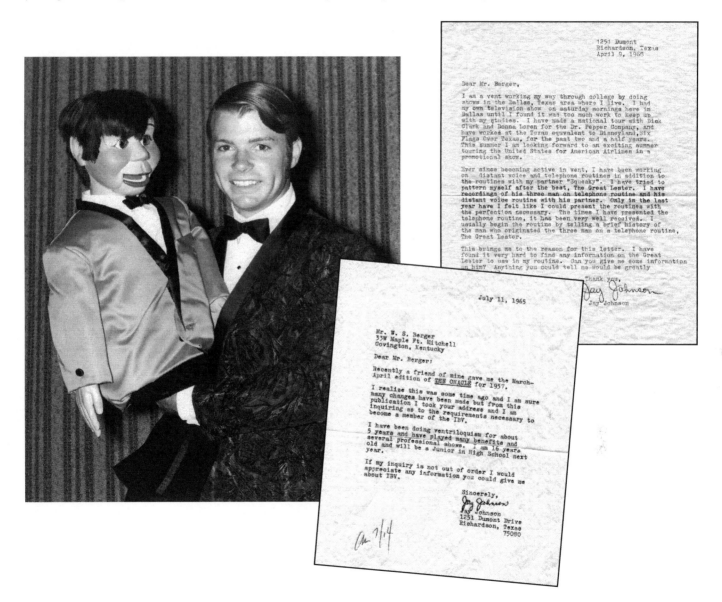

July 12

On this day in 1947, "Crowing Pains,"
a Loony Tunes cartoon, was released by
Warner Bros Pictures. The seven-minute
cartoon centers around Foghorn Leghorn,
Henery Hawk, and Sylvester the Cat along
with Barnyard Dawg, all trying to figure
out who is the real chicken.

Foghorn convinces Henery that
Sylvester is a chicken by using
ventriloquism. Foghorn tells the
audience "You gotta- I say - you gotta
keep on your toes. Toes, that is!"

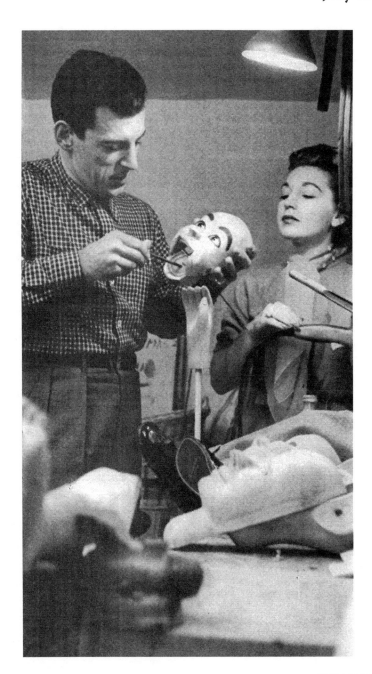

The July 12, 1955 issue of *Look* magazine featured Paul Winchell and arrived in homes today.

The article was entitled, "Paul Winchell: Jerry Mahoney's Star Pupil." In this piece, a 32-year-old Winchell talks about his relationship with his puppet partner Jerry, "He's taught me to think like another person." Ever the innovative thinker, Winchell went on to say, "I aim to prove a divorcement [separation] between two minds. The better the divorcement, the better the act."

July 14

On this day in 1890, Thomas Ferguson (July 14, 1890 – March 17, 1966) was born.

Performing under the name Arthur C. (A. C.) Astor, he was known as "The Globe Trotting Ventriloquist." He toured the world and came to America in 1925. His act was unique, featuring what was called a "sobbing and crying" routine. In short scenes, his partner, "Sentimental Mac," would portray extremely sensitive men while telling a very sad story of lost love or misfortune, sobbing and crying uncontrollably at the end. The routine was not only touching but also comical.

Did you know that on this day in 2011, at the Vent Haven Ventriloquist ConVENTion, the great ventriloquist Jimmy Nelson (December 15, 1928 – September 24, 2019) had a museum building named after him? Vent Haven building Number 4 was renamed "The Jimmy Nelson Building." In addition, Jimmy was bestowed with the title "Dean of American Ventriloquists." It is a title that he carried for the rest of his life.

July 16

Today is ventriloquist Sylvia Cirilo-Fletcher's birthday. Sylvia started performing at age seven, entertaining friends at school with partner Willie. In her freshman year of high school, she ran for class president with puppet partner Leon as campaign manager. Together before the student body they gave their speech which won them the election.

These days Sylvia travels the world performing her own special brand of ventriloquism.

July 17

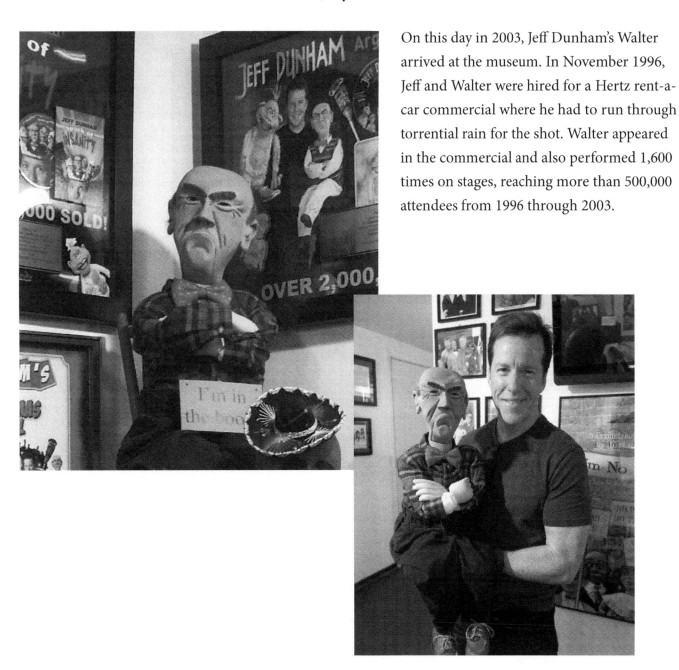

On this day in 2003, Jeff Dunham's Walter arrived at the museum. In November 1996, Jeff and Walter were hired for a Hertz rent-a-car commercial where he had to run through torrential rain for the shot. Walter appeared in the commercial and also performed 1,600 times on stages, reaching more than 500,000 attendees from 1996 through 2003.

July 18

On this day in 2014, Francisco, whose full name is Francisco Gonzalez Garcia de la Garza Gomez Jones (pronounced Ho-nez), found his perch at Vent Haven Museum. He is Sammy King's partner, and the two of them had a 50+ year relationship that began in 1961. Sammy retired after 60 years in show business and in 2014 donated the puppet to the museum during the Vent Haven ConVENTion.

July 19

Did you know that today is the birthday of ventriloquist Richard Potter (July 19, 1783 – September 20, 1835)? Potter, an African American, is the first American born ventriloquist and was extremely popular in the early 1800s.

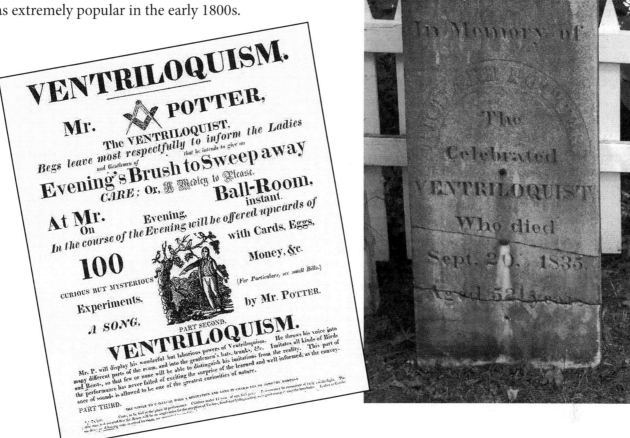

Known as the "Celebrated Ventriloquist," Potter studied under and assisted Scottish ventriloquist and magician John Rannie before branching out on his own when Rannie retired in 1811. Neither Rannie nor Potter ever used a puppet or figure in their act, but instead presented vocal illusions. Potter's ad in 1845 said: "He will throw his voice into many different parts of the room and into gentlemen's hats, trunks, etc."

July 20

Yesterday was the birthday of Venezuelan ventriloquist, Leonardo, the stage name of Horatio Marquez Ortega (July 19, 1904 - May 25, 1983).

He performed with his wife, Ana de Marquez, whose stage name was Anita. His main puppet partner "Maisie" came to Vent Haven Museum in 1985 along with four other figures. Leonardo's act consisted of all five figures, three of which were manipulated by Anita. Maisie is made from paper maché, has freckles, and can blow up a balloon. There are nine Leonardo puppets at Vent Haven.

July 21

On this day in 1924, Jesse Don Knotts (July 21, 1924 – February 24, 2006) was born.

Known on stage as just Don Knotts, the five-time Emmy® winner was not only a terrific comic actor, but also a ventriloquist. His partner's name was Danny "Hooch" Matador. Knotts starred in *The Andy Griffith Show* as well as feature films such as *The Ghost and Mr. Chicken* and *The Incredible Mr. Limpet*. In 1979 *TV Guide* ranked him #27 on its 50 Greatest TV Stars of All Time list.

July 22

It was this week in 1938 that the hands and foot-prints of Edgar Bergen and Charlie McCarthy were immortalized in cement at Sid Grauman's Chinese Theater in Hollywood. Bergen is the only ventriloquist to be honored along with the nearly 200 Hollywood stars including Henry Fonda, Rita Hayworth, Abbott and Costello, Marilyn Monroe, Steven Spielberg, Brad Pitt, Denzel Washington and George Clooney.

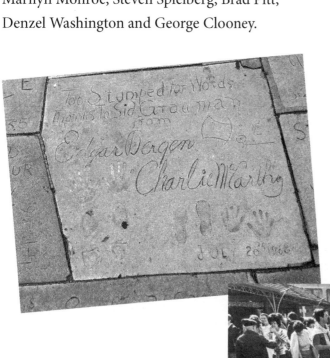

July 23

If it's July, then it's time for the Vent Haven Ventriloquist ConVENTion. Every year, Vent Haven Museum hosts an annual convention for ventriloquists from all over the world. This four-day event began in 1975 and is a family friendly gathering for learning, sharing, and performing.

**1975
VENTRILOQUIST
CONVENTION**

Sponsored by

VENT HAVEN MUSEUM

July 10-12

Drawbridge Rowntowner Motor Inn

I-75 & Buttermilk Pike
Ft. Mitchell, Ky.

When Jay Johnson was 10-years-old, he acquired his first figure. His cousin Judy had a Juro Novelty Company Jerry Mahoney doll that was tucked away in her closet. Judy gave the puppet to Jay and he performed for the family right then and there. He would rehearse for hours on end and got his first paid performance the following spring.

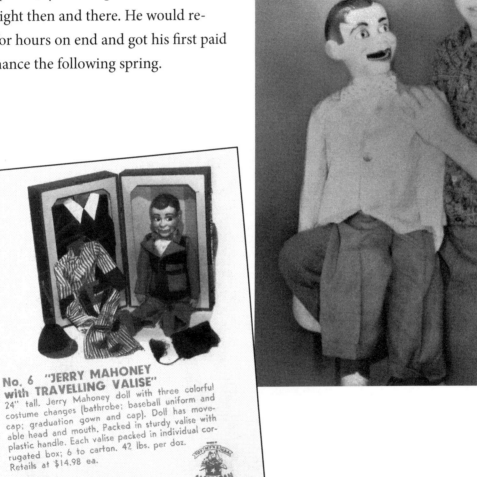

No. 6 "JERRY MAHONEY with TRAVELLING VALISE"
24" tall. Jerry Mahoney doll with three colorful costume changes (bathrobe; baseball uniform and cap; graduation gown and cap). Doll has movable head and mouth. Packed in sturdy valise with plastic handle. Each valise packed in individual corrugated box; 6 to carton. 42 lbs. per doz. Retails at $14.98 ea.

AMERICAN TOYS

JURO NOVELTY CO., Inc., 16 East 18th St., New York 3, N.Y.

British ventriloquist Saveen's main partner, Daisy May, had her own number listed in the London Telephone Directory and children would "ring" her up before they went to school to have a short conversation with her. Daisy May received top billing in larger type above Saveen's name because of her popularity. Misled by her top billing, theater managers would assign a separate dressing room to her and had chocolates and flowers in it. Daisy May had her own bank account with checks made out to her deposited from all of Saveen's performances. Daisy May was also a member of the UK Concert Artistes Association.

July 26

Vent Haven Museum has a unique display celebrating influential figure maker Frank Marshall. The display features carved heads of figures in various states of completion plus tools from his workshop. Marshall's studio was situated at several addresses over the years with his own home basement on South Loomis Street being the final location.

July 27

Today is the birthday of stand-up comic and ventriloquist Stu Gilliam (July 27, 1933 – October 10, 2013). He left home at age 14 to perform with a circus as a ventriloquist, and after a few years began to appear in clubs in Chicago.

In the 1950s and 1960s, he performed in clubs nationwide before black audiences but in southern states was prevented from appearing onstage at the same time as white performers. Eventually, the Playboy Club circuit placed Gilliam all over the U.S. before largely white crowds, which led to him appearing on national television.

July 28

On this day in 1901, Hubert Prior "Rudy" Vallée (July 28, 1901 – July 3, 1986) was born. He was an American singer, actor, bandleader, radio host, and also one of the first modern pop stars who was a teen idol.

But later in life, the crooner took up ventriloquism, adding it to his singing performances. Rudy became so enthralled with the art that he visited W. S. Berger at Vent Haven on several occasions.

July 29

Today is the birthday of Otto Petersen (July 29, 1960 – April 13, 2014). A controversial ventriloquist because of his "blue" act, he performed all over the United States and Canada. Petersen and George, his longtime puppet partner, could be so offensive that after they were the Masters of Ceremonies at the Adult Film Awards (AVN Awards) in Las Vegas, they were not invited back.

He was a regular on the *Opie and Anthony Show* on WNEW and SiriusXM, *The Howard Stern Show* and appeared on the *Late Show with David Letterman*. He was one of the nicest people you could ever meet and loved the art form dearly.

July 30

Did you know that two of Señor Wences' iconic vent partners, Johnny and the boxed head Pedro, "accidentally" came to be?

When Wences was in grade school he was punished for his mischievousness and had to fill the inkwells. He got some ink on his hand, saw the outline of a face, and began working his thumb and forefinger like a mouth – Johnny was born.

On the way to a show in Chicago in 1936, Pedro was riding in the baggage car when the other checked luggage toppled onto his case. The body was smashed beyond repair, and Wences still had to perform, so he salvaged Pedro's head and put it in a box. With that accident, one of the greatest ventriloquist bits was born.

July 31

Ventriloquist Aaron Williams performed on the biggest television shows and on the finest stages around the world, but perhaps his greatest impact on the art form was in 1967 when he joined the Los Angeles County Sheriff's Department.

How About That?: Getting his kicks, elfish dummy Freddy sits on knee of ventriloquist Aaron Williams and digs JET's first hand story of Newark, N. J.'s first Black mayor, Kenneth A. Gibson. Motown star Williams was appearing with Ray Charles at Chicago's Mill Run Playhouse.

He used his skills as a ventriloquist with his puppet partner, Deputy Freddie, to spread the anti-drug and anti-gang messages in person and on television throughout southern California. His signature bit was trying to get a reluctant Freddie back into his case.

August 1

Today is soft puppet maker Mary Ann Taylor's birthday. Currently one of the finest creators of soft puppets, Mary Ann Taylor was drawn to the art form when she saw the work of the legendary Verna Finly at a ventriloquists' convention her husband was attending. Mary Ann was mentored by Verna, and in 1985 began making puppets full time at her MAT Puppets studio.

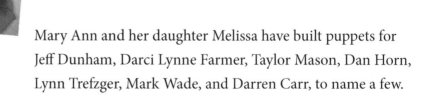

Mary Ann and her daughter Melissa have built puppets for Jeff Dunham, Darci Lynne Farmer, Taylor Mason, Dan Horn, Lynn Trefzger, Mark Wade, and Darren Carr, to name a few.

August 2

Did you know that the original Bob, Jay Johnson's partner, was made by master puppet maker René Zendejas, and then altered by prop master Jack Shafton for the TV show *SOAP*? Jay had the controls adapted to his liking, and Bob is pretty much the same today as when he was originally constructed.

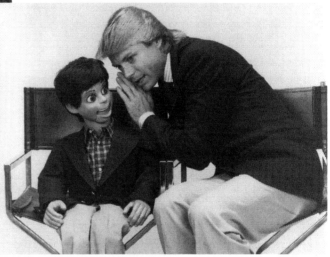

August 3

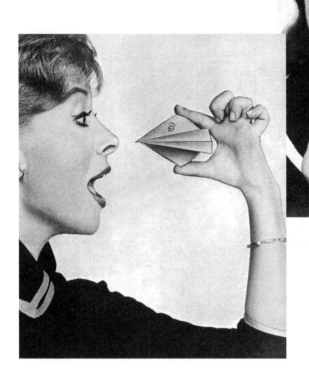

In August 1962, Stein and Day published the book *Folding Paper Puppets*. Shari Lewis and Lillian Oppenheimer co-authored the book that combines the art of puppet making and puppetry with the art of origami. Twenty puppets are featured in the book including Eating Bird, Bloodhound, Fox, Snap Dragon, and Talking Fish.

August 4

On this day in 1966, Willie Tyler and Lester appeared on the music program *Where The Action Is*, a spin off of *American Bandstand* that aired on ABC each afternoon. In this episode, they sang the classic song *Fever*.

August 5

Puppet maker Steve Axtell celebrates his birthday today. Steve is a designer of an amazing array of characters ranging from the most simple to extremely complicated electronic puppets. Steve's creations are used throughout the world.

His company Axtell Expressions has produced more than 100 different characters, some of which are on the cutting edge of technology, utilizing animatronics and remote controls.

240

August 5

Today is the anniversary of Len Insull's (August 5, 1883 – 1974) birthday. Between 1952 and 1974, as Britain's leading and most prolific twentieth century ventriloquial figure maker, Insull produced 2,017 figures. His figures were primarily sold through the L. Davenport and Company Magic shop in London. Noted figures include Lord Charles for Ray Alan, Archie Andrews for Peter Brough, and Hugo Fitch from the film *Dead of Night* (1946), as well as Theo, *I'm No Dummy* alum Stevo Schüling's partner.

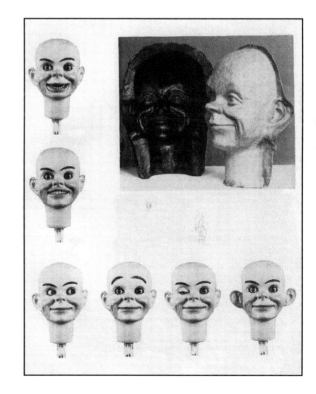

August 6

Did you know that today is film producer Marjorie Engesser's birthday? Marjorie (right), a member of the Producers Guild of America (PGA), produced *I'm No Dummy*, *I'm No Dummy 2*, and *Jay Johnson: The Two & Only!*, amongst other films.

August 7

On this day in 1968, Jimmy Nelson and his wife Betty appeared on *To Tell The Truth* along with Danny O'Day and Farfel. The celebrity panel did not guess the correct "wife" of Jimmy and it was Danny who had to let them know who the real Betty Nelson was.

August 8

Today was the day in 1977 that Jay Johnson had his first of three auditions for the TV series *SOAP*.

OPEN CALL FOR
VENTRILOQUIST
20 to 30 years old
Available for TV series
CBS-TV City
Fairfax & Beverly
Rehearsal Hall Room B-2
Monday, August 8
10 a.m. to 12 noon

His first audition was for casting director Judith Weiner; his second for producers Witt, Thomas, and Harris; and his final audition was for Pam Dixon, Senior VP of Casting for the ABC Television Network.

As reported in the *Chicago American,* ventriloquist Paul Stadelman's partner figure, Winn D. "Windy" Higgins, was a candidate for governor of Kentucky in 1939. On this day, newly elected Governor Keen Johnson sent Windy a letter of thanks. Windy withdrew three months into the race and threw his support to his rival. Nonetheless, Windy received 143 write-in votes. This gubernatorial candidate resides at The Vent Haven Museum and was made by George (Pinxy) Larsen.

August 10

On this date in 1982, Doubleday Balloon Books published Shari Lewis' *One-Minute Bedtime Stories*. It was a collection of 20 one-minute stories including well-known fairy tales, legends, and fables. Shari followed up with several other children's books including *One-Minute Greek Myths*, *One-Minute Christmas Stories*, and *One-Minute Animal Stories*. Shari penned over 60 books, mostly for children.

The bedtime book was released on VHS on August 23, 1989 with Shari, Lambchop, Hush Puppy, and Charlie Horse acting out the stories.

August 11

In 1996, ventriloquist Señor Wences received the "Lifetime Achievement Award" from the National Comedy Hall of Fame for his devotion ''to entertaining generations of audiences and bringing countless hours of joy and happiness to millions throughout the world."

August 12

Ventriloquist Dale Brown performed his own creative twist on the "covered mouth" routine at the 1986 Vent Haven Ventriloquists' Convention. When his version was unveiled, smoking was allowed everywhere at The Drawbridge Inn. Dale and his partner Chip appeared onstage wearing surgical masks in the smoke-filled room, then opened with a rapid-fire exchange. His technique was flawless under the mask.

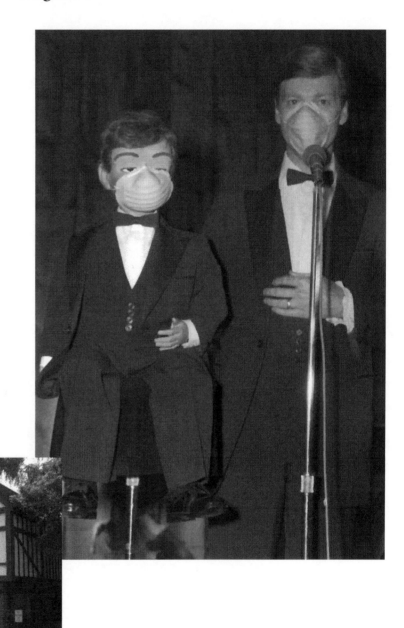

August 13

This month in 1949, Erich Everty's partner Ruland was sent to the Vent Haven Museum. It is most likely the only ventriloquial figure that saved lives.

Everty, who was drafted into the German Army in World War II, was captured on the Eastern Front and held in a Russian prisoner of war camp. In his letter to W. S. Berger, Everty describes how this crude little puppet came to be: "…out of a simple piece of firewood, carved with a poor pen knife, eyes are indicated by pieces of tar and the body was dressed only with a simple piece of paper." According to Everty, he was very proud of his ability to help other prisoners temporarily escape the horrific conditions of their lives through his simple performances with Ruland.

August 14

On this day in 2015, the world premiere of the play *The Ventriloquist Convention* was presented by Halle Puppet Theatre with French/Austrian choreographer, director Giséle Vienne.

Inspired by Vent Haven Museum's Ventriloquist ConVENTion, according to Vienne the play is "an unfolding of various layers of language – speech, gesture, emotion, thought and so on – and we create dialogue through these different linguistic layers." She views puppets as human representations, from sculptures to robots, instilled with the power of metamorphosis.

The Wizard of Oz premiered in Hollywood on this day in 1939. Frank Morgan, who was born Francis Phillip Wupperman (June 1, 1890 – September 18, 1949), portrayed the Wizard and four other characters. He was not only an accomplished and respected actor, but a ventriloquist as well.

Did you know that on this day in 1925, the first significant movie featuring ventriloquism was released? A silent film, *The Unholy Three* starred Lon Chaney as Professor Echo, a ventriloquist. Along with two other circus performers, he commits a series of robberies.

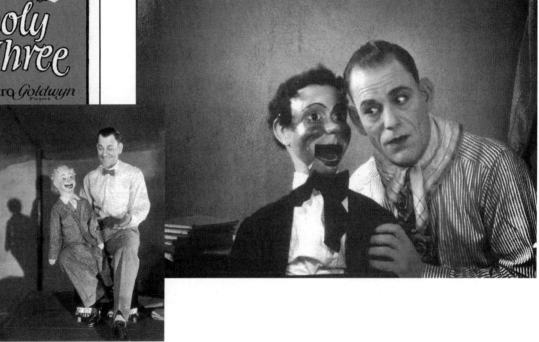

Directed by Tod Browning, *The Unholy Three* was a huge box office success, even though it was a silent film featuring a ventriloquist. It was remade in 1930 with sound, again starring Lon Chaney in his only talkie. Renowned ventriloquist Phil D'Rey coached Lon Chaney in puppet manipulation on both features.

August 17

On this day ventriloquist and co-creator of "The Maher Course of Ventriloquism," Frederick Louis Maher (August 17, 1896 - 1952) was born. Fred was a wonderful ventriloquist and also changed the trajectory of teaching ventriloquism.

According to many sources, Fred and his wife Madeleine opened Maher Ventriloquist Studios in 1934 to supplement their income. They sold "The Maher Course of Ventriloquism," the gold standard of ventriloquism courses for many decades to come. *(continued)*

August 18

"The Maher Course of Ventriloquism" was advertised using small ads and classified advertisements in *Boys Life* and *Popular Mechanics* magazines.

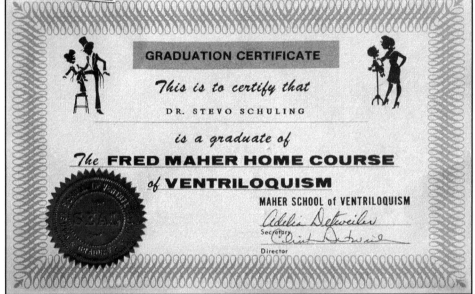

When someone bought the course, Fred would continue the business relationship by offering ventriloquist figures. Madeline Maher was the driving force behind Maher Studios for over 30 years, until Clinton and Adelia Detweiler purchased "The Maher School of Ventriloquism" in 1969 and ran it until 2006. *I'm No Dummy* alum, Stevo Schüling, mastered the craft utilizing this 30-part course.

August 19

In the 1920s, two British ventriloquists vied for the top spot in the field of variety:
Arthur Prince and Tom Coram.

Each man competed on every level and they both had military themed acts. Prince's was naval
and Coram's was army. They both wrote books on ventriloquism and even their billing was a
contest. In 1926, when both arrived in America at the same time to perform in New York City,
Prince was called "The World's Greatest Ventriloquist." Not to be out done, Coram's poster read,
"Greater than the Greatest!"

August 20

On this day in 1957, Shorty Jones began his residency at the Vent Haven Museum. Made in 1908 by Mack and used by Gus Rapp, Shorty is one of the sweetest figures at the museum. So sweet in fact, that when Shorty arrived Gus had included a note that read, "He was a good boy for 50 years. If he talked back it must have been my fault. Give him a nice warm place by the bathroom."

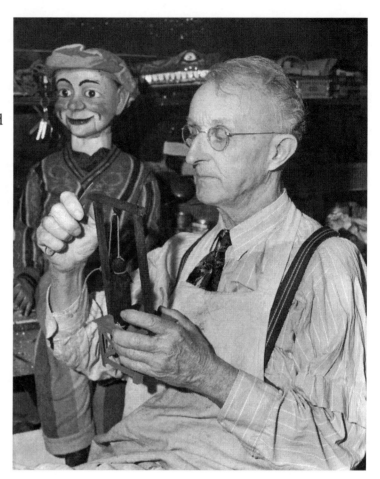

August 21

Today is British ventriloquist Paul Zerdin's birthday. A ventriloquist of international renown, the multi-talented Londoner was 10 when a family friend made him a puppet theatre.

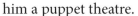

Paul made his TV debut in 1996 as the first winner of London Weekend Television's (LWT) *The Big, Big Talent Show* hosted by Jonathan Ross. He was the winner of 2015 *America's Got Talent* and has headlined his own show at Planet Hollywood Resort and Casino in Las Vegas. His stage show *Paul Zerdin - All Mouth* was filmed in the UK and released on September 13, 2019.

The Juro Novelty Company introduced Hayley O'Hara in 1967.

However, according to Jimmy Nelson, Hayley was a ventriloquial character that "never was real." Juro had Jimmy create the character of Hayley O'Hara to sell with Danny dolls as his "girlfriend" to provide the opportunity for young girls to have a ventriloquist partner. A full-sized figure was never made and Jimmy Nelson never performed with her.

August 23

Shari Lewis took to the podium and conducted symphony orchestras in the United States, Canada, and Japan, offering kid-friendly music, especially the sounds of Beethoven, Bizet, Mozart, and Stravinsky.

During the course of her programs with the symphonies, she danced with showgirl puppets and with a Fred Astaire puppet.

August 24

On this day in 1972, the Vent Haven Museum Board hired its first curator, Susan DeFalaise. There have been five curators and each has used her unique skills to improve the museum. Susan, with the help of the first Advisors' Board, established, directed, and grew the Vent Haven Ventriloquist ConVENTion.

August 25

Today is Timothy T. Miller's birthday. Tim was the executive producer of *I'm No Dummy*, *I'm No Dummy 2*, *Jay Johnson: The Two & Only!* as well as every film produced by Montivagus Productions. He was instrumental in bringing the two documentaries and the Broadway show to the big screen.

August 26

On this day, the United States Postal Service began taking orders for the August 29, 1991 issuing of a 29-cent stamp honoring Edgar Bergen and Charlie McCarthy. Bergen is the only ventriloquist to have his likeness on a stamp. 139,995,600 stamps were issued from Hollywood, California.

August 27

Today is kids' show ventriloquist Mark Wade's birthday. The author of the instructional book *Kid Show Ventriloquism*, he is also Executive Director of the Vent Haven International Ventriloquist ConVENTion. Mark first chaired the convention in 1979 and became the permanent director in 2000.

VENTRILOQUISM
Guess Who's Talking?

DON GAYLORD BRYAN

Don Gaylord Bryan celebrates his birthday today. Bryan has been Canada's premier ventriloquist for almost 40 years. For 35 years, Don's longtime partner and main character has been Mr. Noseworthy, a loveable old curmudgeon. He is a master figure maker as well, and is the author of *Ventriloquism: Guess Who's Talking?*, a how-to-book on ventriloquism and figure making.

August 29

Did you know that today is the birthday of ventriloquist Jay Marshall (August 29, 1919 – May 10, 2005)?

Marshall appeared on the *The Ed Sullivan Show* many times and even filled in as host of the live Sullivan road show, and appeared on nearly every major TV variety hour. His glove-puppet rabbit, Lefty, whose signature song was a sweet and salty version of, "If I Had My Way," often accompanied Marshall. He came up with Lefty during World War II when Marshall used a glove to entertain his buddies. Jay's original Lefty now resides at Vent Haven Museum.

On this day in 1959, this ad with Señor Wences and Johnny appeared in the Sunday editions of newspapers across the country. It would go on to be reprinted many more times for the Scheaffer's Skripriter ballpoint pen back-to-school campaign. The conversation between Johnny and Wences was a play on their iconic bit "Deefeecult."

August 31

During his *I'm No Dummy* documentary interview, Jeff Dunham shared this story. When he was scheduled to perform in Tennessee, his luggage was lost and he was without any of his puppets. Dunham went to Walgreens, purchased a toilet plunger, foam core, construction paper, tape, glue, rubber bands, and markers using them to make a two dimensional José Jalapeno on a Stick for the first performance. That creatively constructed figure now resides at Vent Haven Museum.

September 1

It was this month in 2007 when Jeff Dunham began his *Spark of Insanity* tour.

The tour, which ran through 2010, made Jeff the *Guinness Book of World Records* holder for "Most Tickets Sold for a Stand-up Comedy Tour." Performing in 386 venues worldwide, he appeared in the United States, Canada, England, Sweden, Denmark, Finland, Norway, and Australia.

September 2

Vent Haven's Jacko the Monkey, received by W. S. Berger 1941, is a one of a kind figure constructed by George and Glenn McElroy. His numerous animations include moving eyes that can cross, moving eyebrows, a tongue that sticks out, ears and nose that wiggle, upper and lower curling lips, and a winking mechanism.

Ventriloquists were so enthralled with Jacko that they would ask to borrow him for their act. W. S. was known to be an overly generous man and lent figures to ventriloquists on occasion. As the story goes, W. S.'s wife, Josephine, came up with a novel idea. She bought Jacko for one dollar. Jacko was hers and W. S. never had to say "no" to his friends.

September 3

The first performer recognized as a
ventriloquist was during the reign of
King Francis I of France (1515 – 1547).

Louis Brabant, the valet-de-chambre to the king
and an expert in the art of ventriloquism, deceived
the widowed mother of a young, beautiful and rich
heiress he longed to marry.

Known as the "King's Whisperer," Brabant "could
not only emit a voice from any distance or any
direction, but had, also, the art of counterfeiting any
voice he heard." He calls on the widow, and in front
of several friends and her daughter, in a voice
resembling her husband says, "Give my daughter in
marriage to Louis Brabant! He is a man of excellent
character." Brabant continued to con others through
ventriloquism, making a small fortune.

September 4

This week in 1952, Paul Winchell, Jerry Mahoney, Ted Brown, and Diane Sinclair performed in an extremely clever comedy sketch on the *The Paul Winchell Show* called "The Voice Pill."

In this sketch, Ted tells Paul he has a sore throat and is losing his voice. Paul tells Ted to take a pill that Jerry took earlier. Ted does and when he speaks, he sounds just like Jerry and gets very mad. But when Diane walks by, she sounds like Jerry as well, since she got a pill earlier from Jerry. Paul Winchell did all the voices with perfect timing.

This week in 2014, *Variety Weekly* printed a tribute to ventriloquist Jeff Dunham called "30 Years in Comedy." The article covered Jeff's rise from small comedy clubs to record-breaking performances. Eventually, he sold out sports arenas with many thousands of seats.

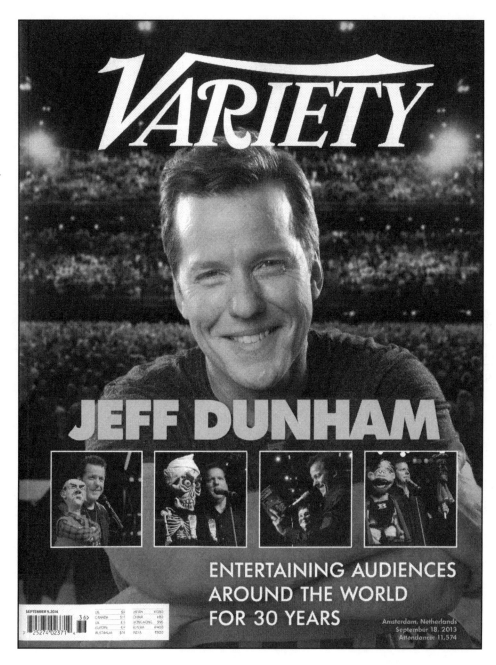

September 6

Today is ventriloquist David Strassman's birthday. An American by birth, now living in Australia, Strassman had a television talk show where his puppet character, Chuck Wood, interviewed celebrities.

In 1986, Strassman added remote control to his figure – utilizing transmitters, motors, and servos. He discovered a remote clutch system in a NASA facility that could be integrated into his own dummies. At the end of Strassman's act, he gets into an argument with his partner and leaves the stage. Sitting alone, Chuck would come to life surprising the audience.

Did you know that Saveen was the first ventriloquist to have a national radio series in Britain? *Midday with Daisy May* was broadcast on the BBC Light Programme right after World War II. Light Programme was a BBC radio station which aired chiefly mainstream light entertainment and music from 1945 until 1967, when it was rebranded as BBC Radio 2.

September 8

Today is the birthday of Willie Tyler. Willie grew up in Southeast Detroit and was shy and withdrawn as a young boy. He watched *The Paul Winchell Show* and thought he could "hide" behind a puppet.

Willie and Lester's act included a musical number. The duo would sing standards and originals.

September 9

Today is The Great Lester's birthday (September 9, 1879 – July 14, 1956, born Maryan Czajkowski in Poland).

Of Harry Lester's many contributions to the art form, one was his innovative stage presence. First, he only worked under extremely bright lights, illustrating his flawless technique. Second, his stage setting was simple: a chair, a small table, a telephone and a decanter of liquor. Third, Lester would often ignore his character, and would even yawn, as he prattled on. Lastly, he would end his act carrying his figure into the audience, because they often thought the puppet was a little person.

September 10

Ventriloquist Billy Joe Boley (September 9, 1935 - December 20, 2000)
was born yesterday in 1935.

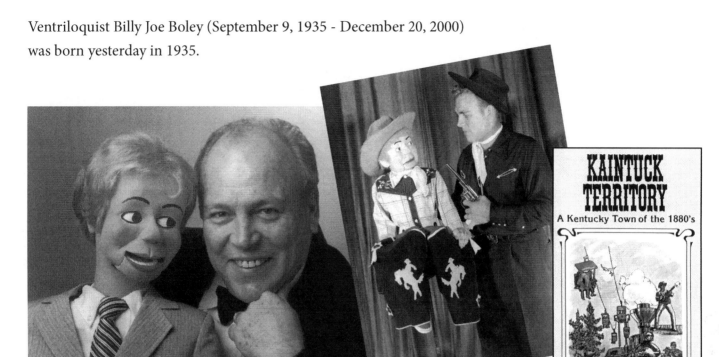

Known as Colonel Bill Boley, his commission came from the title of honor bestowed
by the Governor of Kentucky in recognition of his noteworthy accomplishments and
outstanding service to his community, state, and nation. The Colonel worked for
Carnival Cruise lines for 12 years and was featured at Kaintuck Territory, a western
theme park for 21 years.

September 11

Did you know that Willie Tyler and Lester were regular cast members on the last season of the hit NBC TV comedy *Laugh-In*? The show ran for 140 episodes from January 22, 1968 to March 12, 1973. This date marks Willie and Lester's *Laugh-In* debut.

September 12

On this day in 1929, *The Great Gabbo* starring Erich Von Stroheim was released. It was based on the story *A Rival Dummy* by two-time Academy Award® winning screenwriter Ben Hecht.

Stroheim portrays the brilliant ventriloquist "The Great Gabbo" who increasingly uses his dummy Otto as his only means of self-expression. Gabbo is ultimately driven insane by his work. It is the first time ventriloquism was portrayed as a psychological problem.

September 13

It was on this date in 1982 that the game show *So You Think You Got Troubles?!* premiered with hosts Jay Johnson and Bob.

People with personal problems were interviewed and then offered advice by two professional guest panelists. The contestant would decide which panelist's advice the audience liked more. *(continued)*

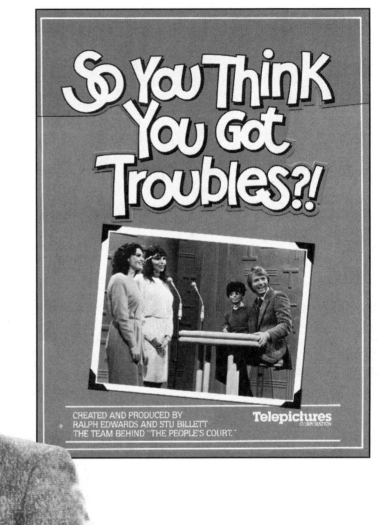

September 14

So You Think You Got Troubles?! opened with this refrain between the announcer and the audience:

Announcer: What do these people have in common?
Audience: Troubles!

Announcer: And what do they talk about when they get together?
Audience: Troubles!

Announcer: And what's the one thing they all say?
Audience: **"So you think YOU got troubles?!**

Announcer: And here's the stars of *So You Think You Got Troubles?!*, Jay Johnson & Bob!

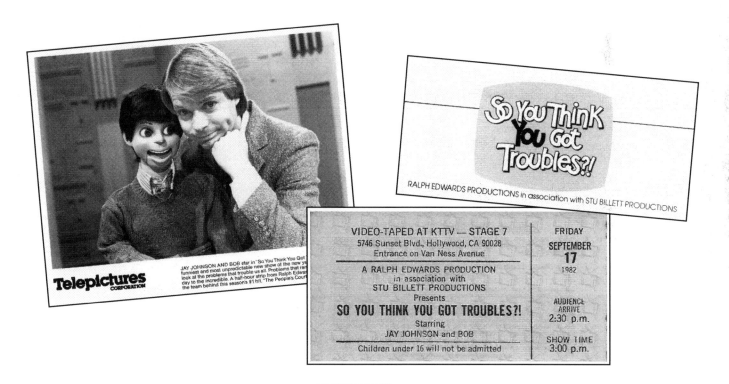

JAY JOHNSON AND BOB star in "So You Think You Got funniest and most unpredictable new show of the new ye look at the problems that trouble us all. Problems that ran day to the incredible. A half-hour strip from Ralph Edwar the team behind this season's #1 hit, "The People's Cour

Telepictures CORPORATION

RALPH EDWARDS PRODUCTIONS in association with STU BILLETT PRODUCTIONS

VIDEO-TAPED AT KTTV — STAGE 7
5746 Sunset Blvd., Hollywood, CA 90028
Entrance on Van Ness Avenue

A RALPH EDWARDS PRODUCTION
in association with
STU BILLETT PRODUCTIONS
Presents

SO YOU THINK YOU GOT TROUBLES?!
Starring
JAY JOHNSON and BOB

Children under 16 will not be admitted

FRIDAY
SEPTEMBER
17
1982

AUDIENCE
ARRIVE
2:30 p.m.

SHOW TIME
3:00 p.m.

September 15

It was on this day in 2012 that the Tony® Award winning Broadway show
Jay Johnson: The Two and Only! was filmed by director Bryan W. Simon
and produced by Marjorie Engesser.

It was filmed with 18 cameras before a live audience at the historic Thalian Hall in Wilmington, North Carolina. Thalian Hall was chosen to shoot the big screen adaptation because it was similar to the Helen Hayes Theater on Broadway where the show originated.

September 16

This week in 1951, the American-Yiddish revue *Bagels and Yox* premiered on Broadway at the Holiday Theater. Ventriloquist Rickie Layne co-starred with partner Velvel. Velvel is the Yiddish name for William. Layne and Velvel also co-starred in the variety review *Borscht Capades* that toured throughout the country.

September 17

This week in 2015, the hit comedy documentary *I'm No Dummy* was re-released in a two-disc set DVD Special Edition with the streaming release following in 2018.

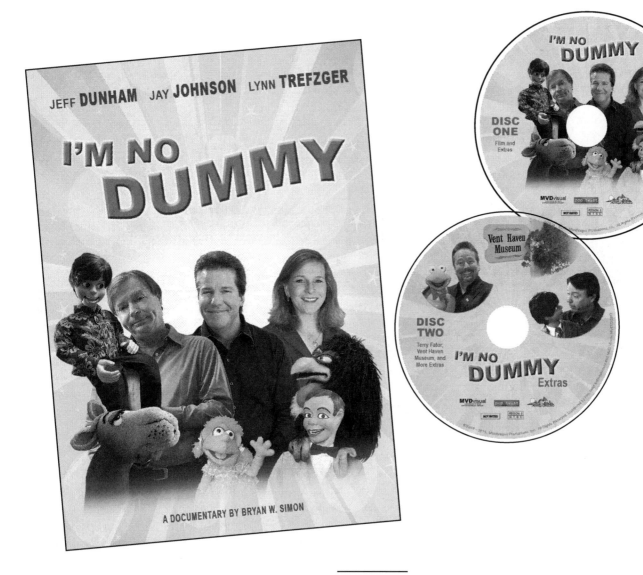

September 18

The Paul Winchell Show premiered on this day in 1950, running in prime time. The series was originally known as *The Speidel Show* until December 1951 when it was renamed for its star. Later, Cheer laundry detergent became the sponsor, and the show was set in Cheerville. The series featured comedy skits, music, and quizzes. It ran through November 20, 1954, then later moved to ABC on Saturday and Sunday mornings with a different format.

September 18

British ventriloquist Raymond (Ray) Alan was born on this day in 1930 (September 18, 1930 – May 24, 2010). Born Ray Whyberd, Alan created extremely memorable characters including Lord Charles, a drunken aristocrat.

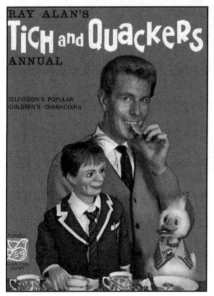

Alan made his television debut with Lord Charles on the BBC program *The Good Old Days* in 1960. The pair was so popular that they performed a record nine times on the show. With two of his other vent partners, he had the successful children's programs *Time for Tich,* and *Tich and Quackers.* In 1986, he presented a television special on Britain's Channel 4 called *A Gottle of Geer.*

September 19

It was during this week in 2006 that *The Late Show with David Letterman* hosted Ventriloquist Week. The five ventriloquists that appeared were Willie Tyler, Jay Johnson, Ronn Lucas, Jeff Dunham and Todd Oliver. Originally conceived as a big joke, the ratings were so high that Letterman scheduled another week beginning February 12, 2007.

Willie's performance included a unique comedy duet with Lester called "The Hambone."

September 20

Did you know that on this day in 2007, Terry Fator became the first ventriloquist to win *America's Got Talent?* For the finale, he, Kermit, and Johnny Vegas performed "You've Got a Friend."

Some of the other songs he performed on *America's Got Talent* were "Friends in Low Places," "Crying," and "I Left My Heart in San Francisco." After winning the show, Terry received one of the largest Las Vegas entertainment deals. Can you name the other two ventriloquists who won AGT? Check out August 31 and October 12 for the answers.

September 20

Come Closer was a game show that premiered on this day in 1954 hosted by ventriloquist Jimmy Nelson and his partners.

Jimmy, Danny O'Day, Humprhey Higsby, and Farfel asked questions of the studio audience. The contestants coming closest to the correct answer won cash and prizes. A jackpot prize, based on a clue given in song by Danny, was also featured. *Come Closer* did not have an advertising sponsor. It was a "sustaining" show. Sustaining shows were shows that were fully financed by the network, in this case ABC. The networks would often charge affiliates a small fee for carrying these shows in order to finance them. *Come Closer* lasted less than a full season.

The Hollywood Chamber of Commerce honored ventriloquist Jeff Dunham with the 2,619th star on the Hollywood Walk of Fame on this day in 2017. One of Dunham's most popular characters, Walter, accepted the star with him. The star, located at 6201 Hollywood Boulevard, is in the category of "Live Performance." Dunham joins ventriloquists Edgar Bergen, Shari Lewis and Paul Winchell. (See February 8 and May 31.)

September 22

Revello Petee (1898 - March 17, 1956) was a renowned figure maker from the 1930s through the 1940s. His father, Julian Petee, began making figures in 1845 in France, and Revello picked up the trade. He made his first figure, Eddie Reed, in May 1907. You can see Eddie Reed at Vent Haven Museum displayed along with several of his other figures.

I. B. V. No. 21

Revello Petee

LIFE MEMBER

Maker of Hand Carved Wood Head Ventriloquial Figures

WRITE FOR PRICES

832 ROBINSON STREET   OROVILLE, CALIFORNIA

Revello primarily sold his figures through the mail from his Oroville, California studio, and sold some figures through Kanter's Magic Shop in Philadelphia and Golden's Magic Wand in Pasedena, California.

September 23

Two favorite figures for Vent Haven curator Lisa Sweasy are
Hedda Wood and Stoney Broke because of "their beautiful faces."

Both are Frank Marshall figures. Hedda came to the museum in 1932, and Stoney arrived in 1984.
W. S. ordered Hedda Wood directly from Frank Marshall's catalog. She cost $50.00 and was one of
the first five figures Mr. Berger purchased. Hedda winks and smokes, and her outfit was made by
Madam Pinxy in August 1937. Stoney was the partner of ventriloquist C. Earle Craig.

September 24

Did you know that on this day in 1950, Jimmy Nelson and Danny O'Day made their national television debut on Ed Sullivan's *Toast of the Town*? Ed declared in his introduction, "A youngster who is the greatest I have ever seen in his field, here is Jimmy Nelson." Jimmy appeared again two months later because his first appearance was cut short. Ed had him back as soon as he could.

A portion of Jimmy's performance was used in *I'm No Dummy*. That clip was taken from a Kinescope, which was the only way to preserve an early television program. A Kinescope is a recording of a television program on motion picture film, directly through a lens focused on the screen of a television monitor.

September 25

Today is ventriloquist Sammy King's birthday.

Born Samuel Leon Faden, Sammy's stage name comes from his mother's family name. He was born in Brownsville, Texas on a huge complex known as Snakeville. His show biz family supplied pet shops, zoos, circuses, and individuals with reptiles, exotic birds, and other animals. Called "The Ventriloquists' Ventriloquist" by his peers, Sammy performed well over 26,000 shows in his 60-year career, perhaps a record. This includes a 20-year run at the Crazy Horse in Paris.

September 26

On this day in 2005, Routledge Publishers released *Art and Ventriloquism* by David Goldblatt.

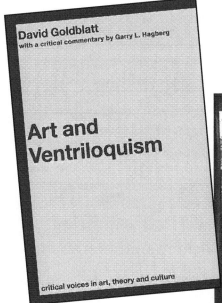

In his book, Goldblatt uses the metaphor of ventriloquism to help understand a variety of art world phenomena. It examines how the vocal vacillation between ventriloquist and dummy works within the roles of artist, artwork, and audience as a conveyance to the audience of the performer's intentions, emotions, and beliefs. In *I'm No Dummy,* he further discusses the relationship between ventriloquist and dummy.

September 27

Modern day ventriloquist Otto Petersen's beginnings in the art form harken back to his predecessors over 200 years earlier. Just as they worked the streets, in front of shops and at fairs, Otto got his start in New York City as a busker or street performer.

He began performing at age seven, dropping out of school at age 13 to hit the streets of Manhattan as well as on the Staten Island Ferry, riding back and forth performing for the commuters.

September 28

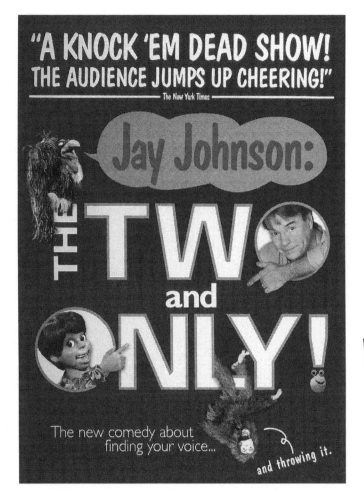

Jay Johnson: The Two and Only!, the Tony® Award winning show written and performed by Jay Johnson, opened on Broadway on this day in 2006 to rave reviews at the Helen Hayes Theatre. Preceded by an acclaimed off-Broadway run at the Atlantic Theatre Company in New York, the show was also performed at the Zero Arrow Theatre, Cambridge, MA, and at the Brentwood and Colony Theaters in Los Angeles. The Cambridge performance garnered the New England Critics Award, and in Los Angeles, Johnson received the 2006 Ovation Award for "Best Solo Performance".

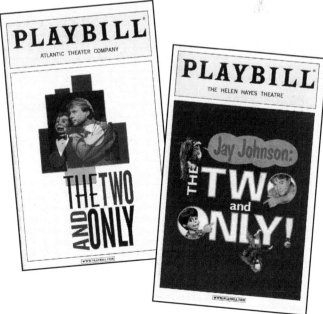

September 29

On this day in 1862, ventriloquist Fred Russell (Thomas Frederick Parnell, September 29, 1862 – October 14, 1957) was born. He and his partner Coster Joe ushered in a more modern style of ventriloquism.

Up until Russell's time, ventriloquists would use multiple figures on stage in a scene or playlet operating the puppets with wires or strings and pneumatic tubes. Russell changed that by working with just one figure and in effect creating a comedy team that is still used today. Because he became the first to introduce a complete music hall act with just one figure, Russell could be considered the "father" of modern ventriloquism.

September 29

Today is the birthday of *I'm No Dummy* associate producer, Tom Ladshaw. An accomplished magician, musician, and ventriloquist, Tom was instrumental in getting the documentary made.

He is a member of the Executive Board of Directors for Vent Haven Museum and is considered one of the foremost authorities on the ventriloquial arts, making him the resident "ventriloquarian."

Ventriloquist Max Terhune's first film was released on this day in 1936. It was *Ride, Ranger, Ride* with Gene Autry, where Terhune portrayed Rufe Jones who has a sidekick named Elmer. Max appeared in over 70 features, almost all of them with Elmer, but his last appearance on the big screen was by himself in *Giant* (1956) as Dr. Walker. It was not only Max's last feature, it was James Dean's as well.

September 30

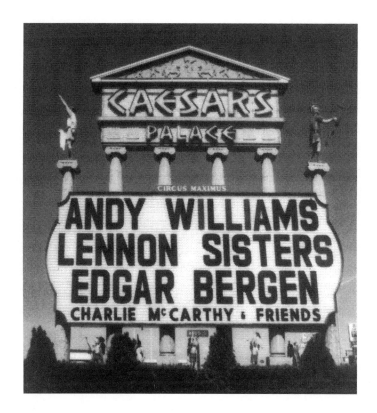

On this day in 1978, Edgar Bergen appeared at Caesars Palace in Las Vegas performing with Andy Williams and the Lennon Sisters.

He got his usual standing ovation and announced his retirement, stating "…every vaudeville act must have a beginning and an end, and that time has come for me, so I'll pack my jokes and my little friends and say goodbye." He left the stage, went to his room at the hotel and quietly died in his sleep, bringing to an end a great show business career.

October 1

On this day in 1960, *The Shari Lewis Show* premiered on NBC Television as part of the Saturday morning color programs. The show ran for three seasons and averaged over 12 million viewers per episode. It was nominated for three prime time Emmy® Awards for Outstanding Program Achievement in the category of Children's Programming, and it won a Peabody Award in 1961.

October 2

TV pioneer John Logie Baird used ventriloquial puppets Stooky Bill and James, on this day in 1925, to transmit the first televised image. Due to the low sensitivity of the photoelectric cells, Baird's first system was not able to televise human faces because they had inadequate contrast, and the lights generated so much heat that he couldn't use a human for testing. Stooky's hair became singed and the painted face cracked from the heat, but they were "the first television actors."

On February 8, 1928, he used Stooky Bill again to transmit the first television image across the Atlantic from London to Hartsdale, New York. Stooky Bill was made by early British figure maker LeMare.

October 2

Did you know that today is the birthday of figure maker Alan Semok (October 2, 1952 – October 27, 2019)?

Known to all as the Dummy Doctor, Alan was a skilled and innovative figure maker. He built puppets for such ventriloquists as Dale Brown, Jeff Dunham, and Lynn Trefzger. Alan also repaired and restored some of the world's greatest ventriloquial original figures. At age 14, he began making figures, selling them through the Flosso-Hornmann Magic Co. Over his lifetime Alan designed and hand-built more than 200 vent figures, hand puppets, and marionettes for professional performers around the globe.

October 3

In 1982, a quiz called, "Name the Dummies?" appeared in newspapers across the country. The *Detroit Free Press* published it in their "The Way We Live" section C.

Name the dummies

Remember Shari Lewis? Paul Winchell? They were among the renowned ventriloquists not so many years ago. Now the tough part: Remember the names of their dummies? Test yourself. Name the dummies who go with the ventriloquists pictured below.

Shari Lewis and ?   Paul Winchell and ?   Edgar Bergan and ?

Jimmy Nelson and ?   Jay Johnson and ?   Willie Tyler and ?   Senor Wences and ?

Answers: 1. Bella   2. Jerry Mahoney   3. Charlie McCarthy 4. Danny O'Day   5. Bob Campbell   6. Lester   7. Johnny

LE
VENTRILOQUE,
OU
L'ENGASTRIMYTHE;

Par M. DE LA CHAPELLE, Censeur
Royal à Paris, de l'Académie de Lyon,
de celle de Rouen, & de la Société
Royale de Londres.

SECONDE PARTIE.

3 liv. les deux Parties brochées.

A LONDRES;
Chez DE L'ETANVILLE, dans James-Street,
New Golden Squarre;
Et se trouve à Paris,
Chez la Veuve DUCHESNE, Libraire, rue Saint-
Jacques, au Temple du Goût.

M. DCC. LXXII.

Ventriloquism really started to take form as an art after French author and former Royal censor of books, Abbé Jean-Baptiste de la Chapelle, conducted a pseudo scientific investigation into ventriloquism. In his 1772 book called *Le Ventriloque, Ou L'engastrimythe* (*The Ventriloquist or the Engastrimth*), he determined that ventriloquism was really a magic trick, rather than a dark art.

October 5

The Vent Haven Museum has approximately 2000
books in their library and archives. The oldest being
that very same 1772 book that was referred to on
October 4.

October 6

Figure makers often used whatever was on hand to create parts for the internal workings of their figures. Frank Marshall used small pieces of plastic for the levers on many of his figures' headsticks and some collectors erroneously believed they were made from chopsticks.

In fact, ventriloquarian Tom Ladshaw discovered that they were made of discarded Bakelite radio fins. Marshall lived around the corner from a radio assembly factory and would gather up the broken and rejected fins, using them for the levers on many of his creations.

The International Brotherhood of Ventriloquists' (IBV) first newsletter was called *The Grapevine News* and was sent out to members from October 1941 through February 1950 when it became *The Oracle*.

THE ORACLE

OFFICIAL PUBLICATION OF THE INTERNATIONAL BROTHERHOOD OF VENTRILOQUISTS

VOL. IX   MARCH-APRIL, 1950   No. 2

Farewell To The Grapevine News

THE ORACLE IS THE NEW NAME OF OUR MAGAZINE
By W. S. BERGER

GUS RAMAGE and JOHNNY JABBERS

hakespeare said: "O. be some ...er name." So we change to a ... appropriate name, The Oracle.

...he name contest came to a close ... the foto which graces this page ...s Ramage, IBV member No. 504 ...axahachie, Texas, who coined ...ew name and received the lar-...number of votes cast by our ...ers.

...analyzing the new name, The ... (of Delphi) was a voice from ...epths guarded by PYTHON, a ...word used for Ventriloquism ... a voice from the belly." The ... has great significance to ...ho guard well the secrets of ...quism.

...ord "engastrimyth" derived ...e Greek, is associated with ...cle and is defined in Web-...ictionary: "A Ventriloquist ...y used of women who deliv-...cles by Ventriloquy."

...r Gus Ramage has been ...g with Johnny Jabbers, ...e Sister, which he present-... Chicago Convention last ...as recently added another ...member to his cast of characters, a small talking doll named "Korki." This doll is parked on the knee of Johnny Jabbers, shown above, he compels "Korki" to do the jabbering,

and finally Tommy Knots will be in the cast, and to say that there will be plenty of rivalry among these wooden head actors, will be putting it mildly.

Gus Ramage is a scholar and a human dynamo. In addition to his show business he has a diversity of accomplishments and responsibili-ties. For his county he is attendance Supervisor for the Schools; proba-tion officer of the County for the County Court; County Librarian; Chairman of the Eye Conservation Committee of the Lions Club; Edit-or of the Lion Log Weekly; he is a minister and preaches every other Sunday; now enrolled in the South-ern University Night School; devotes three hours per week to a course in Criminology in Down Town College in Dallas, Texas; active in Masonic circles, and really finds time to sleep

(Continued on Page 4)

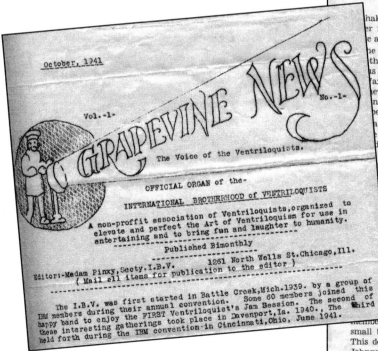

October, 1941

Vol.-1-   GRAPEVINE NEWS   No.-1-

The Voice of the Ventriloquists.

OFFICIAL ORGAN of the-
INTERNATIONAL BROTHERHOOD of VENTRILOQUISTS

A non-proffit association of Ventriloquists, organized to elevate and perfect the Art of Ventriloquism for use in entertaining and to bring fun and laughter to humanity.

Published Bimonthly

                     1261 North Wells St.Chicago,Ill.
Editor:-Madam Pinxy,Secty.I.B.V.
(Mail all items for publication to the editor)

The I.B.V. was first started in Battle Creek,Mich.1939. by a group of IBM members during their annual convention. Some 60 members joined this happy band to enjoy the FIRST Ventriloquist's Jam Session. The second of these interesting gatherings took place in Davenport,Ia. 1940., The Third held forth during the IBM convention in Cincinnati,Ohio, June 1941.

October 8

As a young ventriloquist, Jimmy Nelson entered many amateur shows and contests. It didn't take long before Jimmy won first place on Rubin's *Stars of Tomorrow* show on WGN in Chicago. The popular weekly show was broadcast throughout the Midwest, giving Jimmy some well-deserved recognition.

Jimmy always appeared much younger than his age, as evidenced by this picture taken during the show. He is, in fact, 16 in this photo.

October 9

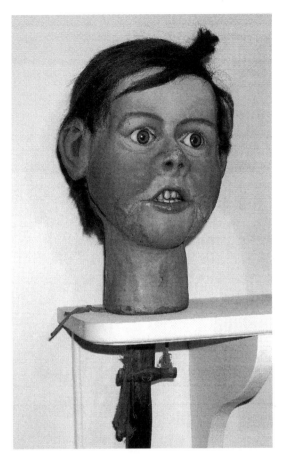

One of the more popular figures used by ventriloquist Walter Hibbert Lambert (see January 9) is Sammy who arrived at Vent Haven on this day in 1951. He is one of the most realistic, photogenic, and show-stopping figures ever to grace a stage.

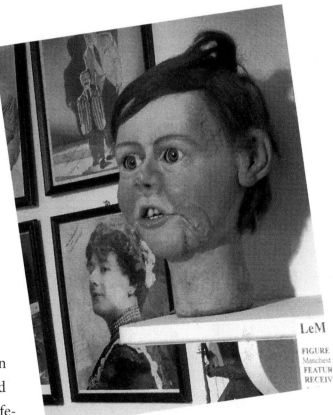

According to curator Lisa Sweasy, Sammy is the most photographed figure at the museum. Close examination of his head reveals his glass eyes, human hair, teeth, and realistic veins painted onto his temples. The head is a life-like model of an actual boy, the son of Lambert's friend. Sammy is more than 100-years old and survived the German Blitz during World War II.

October 10

Walter Hibbert Lambert's plays would last up to twenty minutes.

In *Grandfather,* Lambert plays
the titular role alongside his wife,
Louise (Griffith) Lambert.

In *Artistic Artist*, Lambert as Lydia
Dreams, interacts with two of his figures.

In *His Own Grandfather,* Lambert portrays the title role,
where he beats his grandson. This horrified the audience -
until they realized it was just a puppet.

It was this month in 1981 that Valentine Vox's book *I Can See Your Lips Moving: The History and Art of Ventriloquism* was published in Great Britain. A subsequent condensed German edition was published in 1984, an American edition in 1993, and a Japanese edition in 2003. A revised edition of the book was published on November 1, 2019.

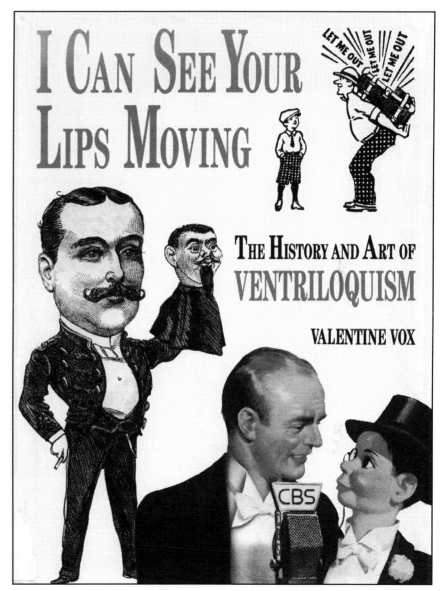

October 12

Today is the birthday of ventriloquist Darci Lynne Farmer. At age 12, Darci Lynne won *America's Got Talent* in 2017 and was runner-up on *America's Got Talent: The Champions* in 2019.

Darci tours the country, makes frequent television appearances, and has had her own television special.

October 13

An animal puppet named Miss Fortune was the first puppet that soft puppet maker Mary Ann Taylor created under the tutelage of her mentor Verna Finly. This clever name and look was inspired by a professor who taught fashion design within the home economics school at Virginia Intermont Girls College where Mary Ann was enrolled. Mary Ann was very fond of her college instructor whose name was, in fact, Miss Fortune.

October 14

Did you know that when The Great Lester retired from performing he opened a school for ventriloquists at 5540 Hollywood Boulevard in Hollywood, California?

It was called Great Lester Studios. He taught the "Lester Method" of ventriloquism, which included breath control, proper diction, manipulation of the figure, and all other facets of ventriloquism. In the mid-1950s, the course cost $300.00. The training board is on display at the Vent Haven Museum.

October 15

Did you know that Albert Saveen was the first ventriloquist to feature a live dog? Saveen had 15 different characters, each with different voices, including a live terrier, Mickey, and a puppet terrier. He would have both the real and puppet dogs on stage at the same time.

October 16

Today is famed British ventriloquist Arthur Worsley's birthday (October 16, 1920 – July 14, 2001). Arthur and partner Charlie Brown had a most unusual routine. Arthur never spoke and Charlie did all the talking.

He was known as "The Mute Ventriloquist" suffering indignity after indignity from Charlie's rapid fire yammering. What made Worsley a genius was that Charlie did all the talking and directed the audience attention to Arthur, making sure they would examine his technique.

October 17

It was on this date in 1961 that W. S. Berger's private collection became Vent Haven Museum. A charter was filed with the Kentucky Secretary of State officially incorporating the not-for-profit museum. The first official meeting of the Vent Haven Museum Board of Directors was held on February 6, 1962. W. S. Berger was elected President; Ventriloquist Tom Farrell, Vice President; and Covington Trust Bank President, Robert H. Taylor, Secretary/Treasurer.

October 18

Released on this day in 1938 in the UK, *The Sidewalks of London* is one of many films that used ventriloquism to advance a plot or a character's back story. On February 15, 1940 the film was released in the United States and renamed *St. Martin's Lane*. The comedy drama starred Charles Laughton as a street entertainer who starts out as a ventriloquist, but evolves into monologues. He teams up with a talented monologist pickpocket played by Vivien Leigh.

October 19

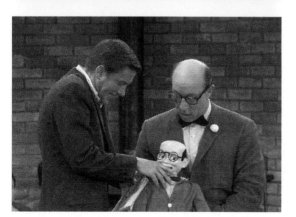

The clichéd bad ventriloquist comedy routine was presented with great success in 1963 on *The Dick Van Dyke Show* in an episode entitled "Too Many Stars." During this show Mel Cooley, portrayed by Richard Deacon, auditions for the community talent show with his wooden partner, a Jerry Mahoney puppet reconfigured to look like Mel. He is a terrible ventriloquist, and when Dick Van Dyke as Rob Petrie comments on his lip control, Mel says "Well, they're better than they used to be." The episode aired on October 30, 1963 on the CBS Network.

October 20

Shari Lewis introduced sock puppet Lamb Chop on the *Captain Kangaroo Show* on this date in 1956. Previously, Shari used traditional hard figures like Samson and Buttercup. (See February 4th.)

This led to her own television show, *The Shari Show.* She appeared two more times on the *Captain Kangaroo Show*, March 2 and July 24 in 1957.

October 21

Willie Tyler and Lester appeared on the *Flip Wilson Show* on this date in 1971.

On Season 2, Episode 6 Willie and Flip did a ventriloquist routine in which Lester meets his sister. Willie had a back-up Lester that he was not using because it didn't look quite right, so they used that figure to portray Lester's sister. Flip hid his mouth behind the puppet and manipulated it and Willie worked Lester. The routine was a huge success.

October 22

The Jeff Dunham Show premiered on this day in 2009 on Comedy Central.

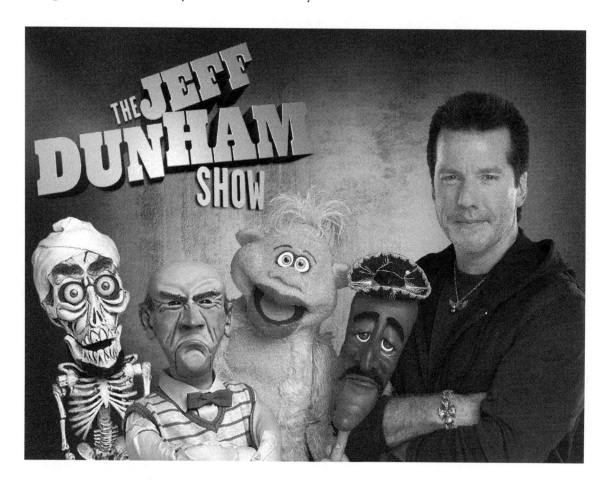

The show was a sketch comedy series featuring Dunham and his characters (Walter, Achmed the Dead Terrorist, Peanut, Bubba J, José Jalapeño on a Stick, and Sweet Daddy Dee). They performed routines in front of a studio audience mixed with previously recorded segments where the characters visited real people and places around Los Angeles. The show ran for one season. The series' final episode aired on December 10, 2009. The show was released on DVD May 18, 2010.

October 23

John William Carson (October 23, 1925 – January 23, 2005) was an American television host, comedian, writer, and producer. He began his career in entertainment as a magician and ventriloquist.

But best known as the host of *The Tonight Show Starring Johnny Carson* (1962–1992), Carson received six Emmy® Awards. He was inducted into the Television Academy Hall of Fame in 1987. Carson was awarded the Presidential Medal of Freedom in 1992 and received a Kennedy Center Honor in 1993.

October 24

Today is the birthday of German ventriloquist Dr. Stefan Schüling who appeared in *I'm No Dummy*.

Known on stage as Stevo, he ran the only school in Germany dedicated to teaching ventriloquism. People from all over the world attended his school in Münster to learn Die Kunst des Bauchredens or The Art of Ventriloquism.

October 25

Ventriloquist Louis McBride (October 25, 1904 – June 6, 1983) was born today. His partner's name was Silas.

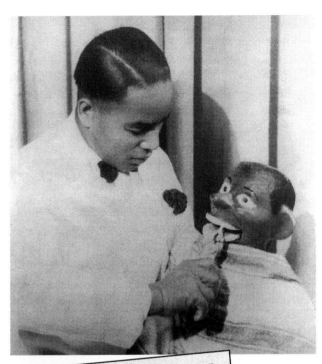

FOR WORTH-WHILE ENTERTAINMENT!

Add That Final Touch, Something Unusual...

McBRIDE

The World's Greatest Ventriloquist and Magician

Offers Entertainment that is truly unique,
for Parties, Clubs, Churches, Banquets
or any Public or Private Affairs

You'll be amazed at the Reasonable Rates!

WIRE or WRITE

Fifteen Minutes or an Hour, Your Option.

McBRIDE, The Magician
DISTINCTIVELY DIFFERENT

Phone..................

Louis was a popular ventriloquist. The highlight of his act was when he pulled an aching tooth from Silas' mouth. The punch line was that it was the wrong tooth. In December 1949, *Ebony* magazine featured McBride and Silas.

October 26

Today is ventriloquist Megan Piphus' birthday. Megan was a contestant on season eight of *America's Got Talent* with her characters Princess and Monica. In 2020 Piphus joined the cast of *Sesame Street* as the voice of Gabrielle. Prior to her AGT appearance, Piphus appeared on *The Oprah Winfrey Show*, where she was featured on "Oprah's Search for the World's Smartest and Most Talented Kids" and also appeared on *The Tonight Show* with Jay Leno, and FOX's *Showtime at the Apollo*.

Megan graduated valedictorian of her class at Princeton High School and her graduation speech featured her puppet. She became known as the "Valedictorian Ventriloquist." Blending her vocal prowess with ventriloquism, Megan captivates audiences of all ages through comedy, impersonations, musical anecdotes, and inspirational messages.

October 27

Tomorrow is the birthday of ventriloquist Herman Stoike (October 28, 1883 – November 1, 1951). Known as Uncle Herman, Stoike was also a Chicago police officer who was in charge of the lock-up at the Damen Avenue Station.

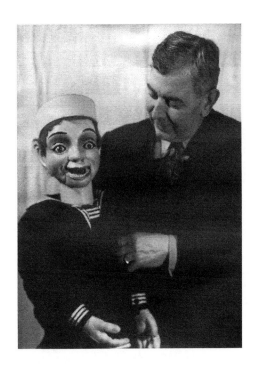

More importantly, it was Herman Stoike who selflessly mentored Jimmy Nelson, helping the aspiring ventriloquist to begin developing the "proper" techniques. Without Uncle Herman, there would not have been a great Jimmy Nelson.

Uncle Herman & Eddie

October 28

Today is the birthday of ventriloquist William F. Holliday (October 28, 1912 – November 15, 1970). William was known as "Bill Holliday, America's Finest Colored Ventriloquist." He also used the taglines "A Surprise A Minute" and "The Vent Act That's Different" in his advertisements.

He learned the art form through the Maher correspondence course. His wife, Jean Idelle, was a burlesque star known as "The Sepia Sally Rand." She was inducted into the Burlesque Hall of Fame in 2012 in Las Vegas.

October 29

On this day in 1960, the Associated Press distributed a 50-word article to nearly 2,000 newspapers across the country entitled *Ventriloquism Exposed*. It was published the following day.

Throwing Voice Is No Trick At All

LITTLE ROCK, Ark. (AP) —There is no such thing as "throwing your voice," says night club ventriloquist Peter Rich.

"It's 90% acting and 10% ventriloquism," he adds. "I just talk without moving my lips and attract people's attention to my dummy."

Rich said anyone could learn the trick by practicing 10 minutes a day.

Ventriloquist Peter Rich, who was performing in Little Rock, Arkansas, was the focus of this article that stated, "There is no such thing as throwing your voice, says night club ventriloquist Peter Rich." It goes on to say, "Rich said anyone can learn the trick by practicing 10 minutes a day."

October 30

Today is the birthday of renowned ventriloquist Rickie Layne (October 30, 1924 - February 11, 2006). Rickie, born Richard Israel Cohen, and his Yiddish partner Velvel, first appeared on the *The Ed Sullivan Show* on January 1, 1956. They appeared another 47 times over the years.

Rickie and Velvel were regulars on the Borscht Belt comedy circuit until singer Nat King Cole saw his act at Ciro's on L.A.'s Sunset Strip. Cole was so impressed, he urged Ed Sullivan to book Rickie and Velvel. His grave marker says "One Lucky Guy!!."

October 31

Did you know that today is ventriloquist Shirley Dinsdale's birthday (October 31, 1926 – May 9, 1999)? After being badly burned in a household accident when she was 5-years old, she was given a ventriloquist's dummy by her father as part of her recovery. He manufactured dummies for department stores.

PROGRAMS for WEEK BEGINNING DECEMBER 6th

RADIO *life*

3¢ WEEKLY

Rival for Bergen?
Story on Page 33

She named her new figure Judy Splinters, and at age 15, Dinsdale got her own radio show entitled *Judy in Wonderland* on KGO in San Francisco. At age 23, she won the very first Emmy Award (See January 25th).

November 1

The hit comedy series *SOAP* premiered on September 13, 1977, but it wasn't until episode 7 on November 1, 1977 that characters Chuck Campbell and Bob arrived from Hawaii.

Jay Johnson and Bob were so popular that a four-episode arc turned into 59 episodes. Jay's role on *SOAP* would forever change the modern day trajectory of ventriloquism.

November 2

This is the day in 2010 when Jeff Dunham's autobiography, *All By My Selves: Walter, Peanut, Achmed and Me*, went on sale.

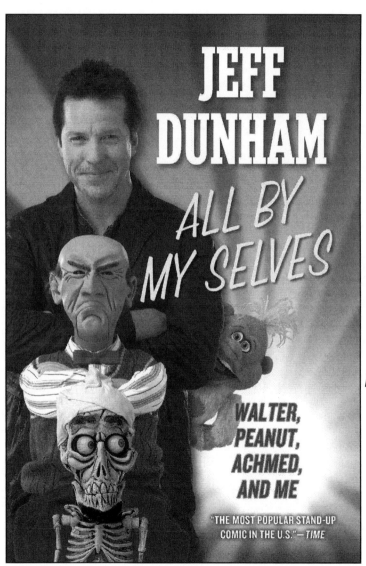

A *New York Times* best seller, the book chronicles the long and winding road to becoming one of America's favorite ventriloquists.

November 2

Figure maker Glenn McElroy (November 2, 1910 - November 28, 1991) was born on this day.

He and younger brother George produced some of the most remarkable figures ever made. The figure used in the 1978 feature film *Magic* starring Anthony Hopkins was based on the McElroy style. Glenn McElroy was responsible for the elaborately detailed mechanics inside the legendary figures.

November 3

It's the time of year for presidential elections and one ventriloquist definitely embraced the political process, dummy wise. In August 2016, Jim Teter's nine presidential figures arrived at Vent Haven Museum in Jim's car. Seven of the figures are on display.

Teter performed in over 50 countries with his figures and at the White House for Presidents Ford, Nixon, and Eisenhower as well as at a White House Correspondents Dinner. He was an excellent mimic of the Presidents' voices and mannerisms. The wooden heads of state were the primary focus of Teter's act for over 50 years and each wears the presidential pin from their administration.

November 4

In the 1970s, Shari Lewis added another dimension to her act by moving to more adult stages such as Las Vegas show rooms and other venues.

November 5

Did you know that Edgar Bergen's last name was actually Berggren?
Johan and Nilla Berggren's boy, Edgar, learned ventriloquism from
Herrmann's Wizards' Manual.

After developing his skill, Edgar hired Chicago woodcarver Theodore Mack to fashion the
head of his life-long sidekick. The likeness was based on a precocious Irish newsboy. Bergen
entered Northwestern University, performing with Charlie McCarthy to pay the bills. While
on vaudeville, he changed his name to the easy- to-pronounce Edgar Bergen.

November 6

Today is the birthday of figure maker Tim Selberg. Tim creates handcrafted and custom carved puppets for collectors and entertainers.

His work can also be found in museums and private collections around the globe. In 1986, Tim started making figures full-time for his Selberg Studios and today makes Living Puppets that are extremely lifelike, Extreme Puppets which have exaggerated and bold facial features, and Custom Figures that are made to order.

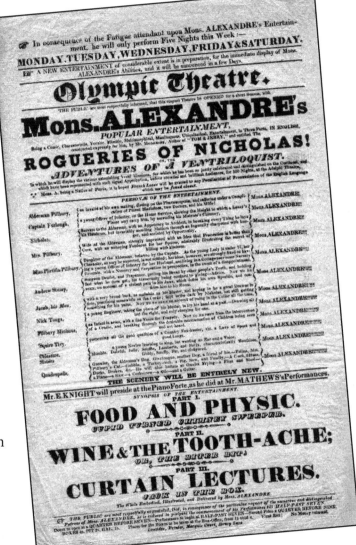

On this date in 1796, Nicolas Marie Alexandre Vattemare (November 7, 1796 – April 7, 1864) was born. He was known as Monsieur Alexandre as a boy. His mother sent him to the seminary to be educated, but he was expelled for performing ventriloquism. In 1815, while working as a nurse in Berlin, he amused the patients with ventriloquism so well that the doctors advised him to perform professionally. He took their advice, and toured throughout Europe, becoming rich and famous. He donated generously to charitable organizations.

(continued)

Monsieur Alexandre was the first ventriloquist to cause a sensation worldwide. The admirers of his ventriloquial skills included the Marquis de Lafayette, the Dowager Queen of England, and the Archbishop of Canterbury. His popular program was called *Adventures of a Ventriloquist or The Rogueries of Nicholas*. He did not use any figures which was the tradition of the time. Instead, he had conversions with a dizzying array of persons and animals, all vocally portrayed by himself. He was the inspiration for the 1840 Victorian novel, *The Life and Adventures of Valentine Vox the Ventriloquist* by Henry Cockton that introduced a whole new audience to the art form.

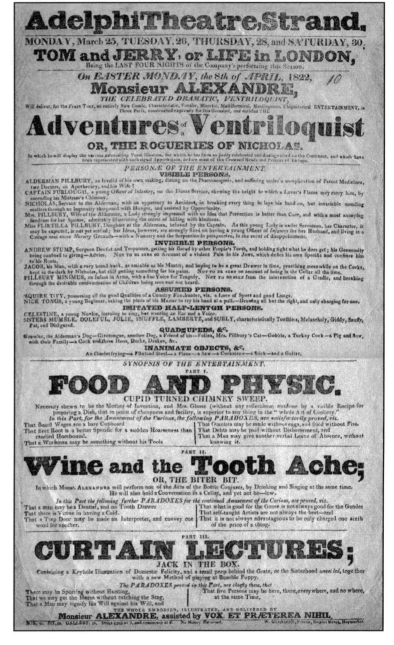

November 9

In 1923 at the Liford Hippodrome Theatre in London, the most spectacular and amazing display of ventriloquism ever staged was unveiled. More than one year in the making, Fred Russell presented "Sylvester vs. Fitzcholmondely" in a scene called *Breach of Promise*.

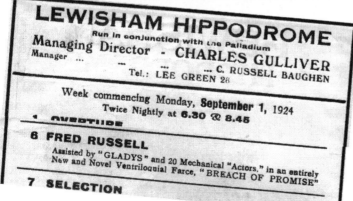

The play portrayed an English trial with 20+ characters involving a damage suit for 5,000 pounds. Portraying the lawyers, Russell and his wife were the only humans on stage. Russell controlled the "cast" with pneumatic tubes connected to foot pedals that he manipulated. The play was a sensation and toured for three years.

November 10

The first magazine/newsletter for ventriloquists was issued in November 1937. Published by figure maker Revello Petee, *Double Talk: The Ventriloquist's Guide*, was very clear in its mission: "No contributions on magic accepted."

There have been many other bulletins such as *The Oracle* (1950-1960), *VENT-O-GRAM* (1963-1969), *Distant Voices* (1997-2003), *Ventriloquists Guild Journal* (1986-1999), *Dialogue* (1981-1999), but it was Petee who began connecting ventriloquists via a publication. The pictured newsletters are archived at Vent Haven Museum.

November 11

This week in 1978, the feature film *Magic* was released in theaters. In the film a ventriloquist, portrayed by Anthony Hopkins, tries to rekindle a romance with his high school sweetheart only to be thwarted by his vicious dummy. The voice of Fats was performed off screen and the dummy was created to look similar to Hopkins in a McElroy figure-style. The film was directed by two-time Academy® Award winner Lord Richard Attenborough with a screenplay by double Oscar® winner William Goldman based on his novel of the same name.

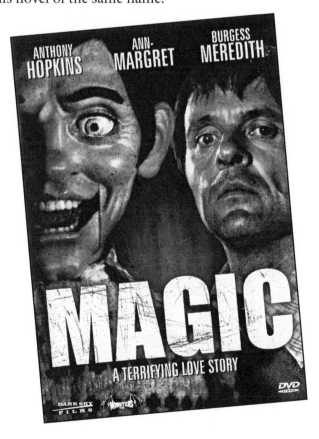

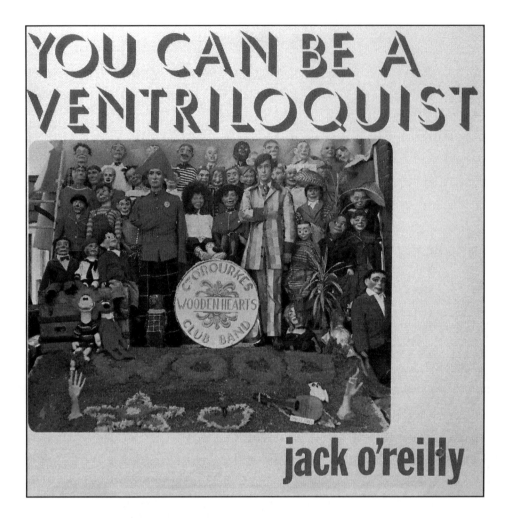

The L.P. "You Can Be A Ventriloquist" was released in 1968 on the Saga Label by Valentine Vox under his previous stage name Jack O'Reilly.

The cover picture is a pastiche of the Beatles' "Sgt. Pepper's Lonely Hearts Club Band" album front. The "drum" has "Constable O'Rourke's Wooden Hearts Club Band" written on it. Right of center is Jack in front of the ventriloquists' figures. Record producer Ken Warriner suggested the recording begin with a lesson about the history of ventriloquism. This suggestion inspired Vox to write the book *I Can See Your Lips Moving*, a history of the art form.

November 13

Early in Shari Lewis' career she recorded albums, mostly for children, which continued throughout her lifetime. By all accounts, Shari released 17 albums and 45s. They included *Gotta Have Rain*, *Shari in Storyland*, *Some Things for Xmas*, *Jack and the Beanstalk*, and others.

November 14

Soft puppet makers Mary Ann and Melissa Taylor (MAT Puppets) create over 50 puppets a year. No two puppets are alike. It can take six to eight months to create the final puppet, from concept to finished product. Verna Finly and the Muppets have influenced their style.

November 15

Animal figures are common in the world of ventriloquism. Three unusual figures that reside at the Vent Haven Museum are the kangaroo trio: Katie, Kangaroo, and the little Joey (in Katie's pouch). Australian ventriloquist Clifford Guest had Frank Marshall construct the puppets for him. Guest used Katie when he appeared on *The Ed Sullivan Show*. He eventually sold them to W. S. Berger, who made them part of the Vent Haven collection.

November 16

Jeff Dunham's sixth special, *All Over the Map*, premiered
on Comedy Central on this day in 2014.

The show was taped in several countries, including: Ireland, Iceland, Norway, the United Kingdom,
United Arab Emirates, Israel, and South Africa. For one television special, airing in Malaysia, Achmed
the Dead Terrorist was temporarily renamed 'Jacques Merde, the Dead French Terrorist.' Feel free to
Google "merde."

Did you know that today is legendary British ventriloquist Arthur Prince's (November 17, 1881 – July 14, 1946) birthday?

In 1912, Prince appeared before King George V in the first Royal Command Performance. Prince and partner Jim toured the world with their comedy act 'Naval Occasions'. In the act, Prince wore a naval officer's uniform while Jim was dressed as a jolly Jack Tar with the words "H.M.S. Prince" on the band of his cap.

November 18

Ventriloquarian Tom Ladshaw has authored over 20 instructional and performance books, and several biographies. Some of his books include *The Really Big Book of Hilarious Comedy Material for Ventriloquists: (and Other People Who Like Books with Long Titles Containing the Word "Ventriloquists")*, *The Magical Ventriloquist*, and *A Jimmy Nelson Celebration: 70 Years of Laughter*.

In addition, Tom is the certified appraiser for ventriloquism-related donations to Vent Haven Museum.

November 19

Did you know that tomorrow is ventriloquist Bill DeMar's (November 20, 1931- February 11, 2015) birthday?

Born William Crowe, Jr., Bill was scheduled to appear as master of ceremonies at Jack Ruby's Carousel Club in Dallas the night President John F. Kennedy was assassinated. In turn, Jack Ruby was the one who gunned down the President's assassin, Lee Harvey Oswald. The Warren Commission and CBS's Dan Rather interviewed DeMar after his employer shot Oswald.

On this date in 1944, Edgar Bergen was featured on the cover of *Time* magazine. Bergen is arguably the most famous ventriloquist. At the height of his career, he and Charlie McCarthy were as well known around the world as presidents, popes, and movie stars.

November 21

On this day in 1941, the RKO film *Look Who's Laughing* was released starring Edgar Bergen and Charlie McCarthy. Lucille Ball co-stars with Bergen and McCarthy. In this film, Bergen and McCarthy perform a doctor's sketch they originated on stage.

1941, Steven Spielberg's cult comedy film, was released in December 1979. In the film, Herbie (Eddie Deezen), has a ventriloquist dummy with him while he's perched atop a Ferris wheel on Santa Monica Pier looking out for approaching Japanese planes. Ventriloquist Jerry Layne manipulated the puppet and performed the voice.

November 23

On this date in 1980, Señor Wences was the special guest on *The Muppet Show* in the UK. This episode, Number 508, did not appear on American television until May 30, 1981, although it was produced a year earlier. Wences appeared with Johnny, Pedro and Cecelia, did a telephone routine and spun plates. He was 84 years old when the show was taped by Associated Television (ATV) at Elstree Studios in England.

November 24

On this day in 1990, *Broken Badges* premiered on CBS Television starring Jay Johnson and Bob. The Steven J. Cannell cop series also starred Miguel Ferrer, Ernie Hudson and Eileen Davidson. A former New Orleans detective recruits a group of misfit Los Angeles cops forming them into a separate crime-fighting unit.

Jay portrayed Officer Stanley Jones and Bob portrayed his partner Danny. The part was specifically written for Jay and Bob by co-creator Randall Wallace. When the series was released in March 1992 in Germany, it was called *Das Psycho-Dezernat* which translates into The Psycho-Department.

November 25

The Nestlé's Quik commercials starring Jimmy Nelson, Danny O'Day, and Farfel were originally filmed live. Later, the commercials were taped, allowing for more exciting scenarios where Danny might be an astronaut or a racecar driver.

Jimmy always did the voices but wanted the characters to appear to move independently. Ray Austin, an excellent figure manipulator, was the primary puppeteer.

November 26

Tomorrow, November 27th, is the birthday of Buddy Big Mountain. This groundbreaking Native American ventriloquist is known as "North America's Aboriginal Original." As a member of the Iroquois Nation and a registered member of the Mohawk Kahnawake Tribe of Canada, Buddy brings the culture, characters, and dialog of his heritage to audiences all over the world.

November 27

On this day in 1931, John R. S. Brooking
(November 27, 1931 - December 24, 2006)
was born.

Very few non-ventriloquists have made such an impact on the art form as Mr. Brooking. He was
W. S. Berger's friend and attorney who successfully transitioned and guided W. S.' collection into the
museum we know today. Brooking's steadfast leadership is why the museum collection was never
destroyed or liquidated and may still be enjoyed by all.

November 28

On this date in 1983, Ronn Lucas' television special
Who's in Charge Here? was released.

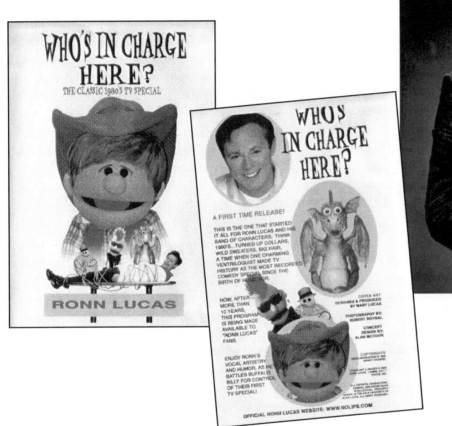

The CBC/The Disney Channel television production filmed in Canada before
a live audience starred Lucas' puppet partners including Buffalo Billy and Chuck
the punk rocker. Ronn also shows the audience how to make puppets out of socks
and random objects. *Who's in Charge Here?* was nominated for a CableACE award.

November 29

There are countless stories of ventriloquists using their skills to con or play tricks.

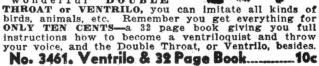

Like some, Louis Brabant (See September 3) used ventriloquism for nefarious purposes to con innocents. Saint-Gille was rumored to make a dead monk speak to his brothers in a not so delicate trick. Monsieur Alexandre made a dead fish reply, "It's a damn lie," when a fishmonger claimed it was fresh. There are stories about young vents who used their skill to call them out of class over the PA system. Others tell of mimicking a police siren to scare away a mugger.

One of the many fascinating files in Vent Haven Museum's library is a collection of ventriloquist-related sheet music. Morton Gould's "The Ventriloquist" for piano solo (1939) and Benjamin Rungee's "The Talking Dummy" for piano solo (1944) are just two of them. The Grammy, Pulitzer, Kennedy Center, and Drama Desk award winning Gould (December 10, 1913 - February 21, 1996) was prolific, having composed around 150 works.

ARTHUR PRINCE
AND JIM

When British ventriloquist Arthur Prince passed on
July 14, 1946, he received much adoration. His many fans
paid a shilling each to the undertaker to view his body in the
chapel. After almost five decades of performing as a team,
Prince and his partner Jim were buried together.

December 2

During this month in 1961, Shari Lewis and Lamb Chop were hired to present a holiday message sponsored by the National Association of Theatre Owners. The short film was screened before the main attraction in theaters across the country. This heartfelt message ran December through January for the 1961-1962 season.

December 3

Did you know that today marks the anniversary of ventriloquist Harold Crocker's 1960 appearance on the *Ted Mack Original Amateur Hour*?

Crocker's performance on this variety show was delightful. He is one of the most affable people one could meet. Decades later, Harold and Butch are still performing together.

December 3

On this day in 2014, the big screen adaptation of the Tony Award® winning Broadway show *Jay Johnson: The Two & Only!* had its theatrical world premiere at the historic Egyptian Theater in Hollywood. Following the screening, a lively Q & A with Jay Johnson and Bob, producer Marjorie Engesser, and director Bryan W. Simon was hosted by Christopher Lockhart. The DVD premiered just two weeks later on December 16.

In a twist on what Hollywood calls the "distribution waterfall," the theatrical release for *Jay Johnson: The Two & Only!* came after the pay-per-view television premiere which began four months earlier on August 9, 2014.

Beginning this month in 1951, Edgar Bergen and Charlie McCarthy flew to Army, Navy, and Air Force hospitals bringing gifts to wounded veterans of the Korean War and presenting a show. In April 1952, they received the Air Force Citation of Merit in Washington, D.C., and in 1953, the United States House of Representatives honored Edgar Bergen for his program *Operation Santa Claus*.

Flying Funnyman

by EDWARD CHURCHILL

Edgar Bergen is famed only as a ventriloquist, yet the aviation industry could use a hundred like him. He is an air-minded gentleman with plenty of ideas.

December 5

Did you know that ventriloquist Ronn Lucas
portrayed Willie Ward in the episode "Willie Ward"
(Season 4, Episode 14) of the TV series *Nip/Tuck*?

The episode aired on December 5, 2006. In a concept right out of *The Twilight Zone*, a ventriloquist
who's no longer in demand asks a plastic surgeon to make him look like his puppet partner. The
ventriloquist has aged, but the puppet obviously hasn't.

December 6

Tomorrow is the birthday of Ted Knight, born Tadeusz Wladyslaw Konopka (December 7, 1923 – August 26, 1986). He began his acting career as a ventriloquist.

Knight, known for his Emmy® award-winning portrayal of Ted Baxter on *The Mary Tyler Moore Show*, was the first professional ventriloquist Jay Johnson saw perform live. Jay was just 11-years-old when his father took him to see Knight. After the performance Jay spoke with him and Knight demonstrated how the two figures worked.

December 7

"Museums for $1200, Alex."
On this day in 2020, Vent Haven Museum was featured on the *Jeopardy!* game show hosted by Alex Trebek.
Answer: "Vent Haven Museum in Fort Mitchell, Kentucky is dedicated to the art of using these puppets, like Charlie McCarthy."
We hope by now you know the question.

VENT HAVEN MUSEUM IN FORT MITCHELL, KENTUCKY IS DEDICATED TO THE ART OF USING THESE PUPPETS, LIKE CHARLIE MCCARTHY

Question: What is ventriloquism?

December 8

W. S. Berger was the heart and soul of the ventriloquist community from the 1930s until his passing in 1972. He wrote and received hundreds of letters a month with advice and encouragement to ventriloquists all over the world.

He was revered by so many that if there were a dispute or feud between professionals in the art, he would be called upon to negotiate a settlement between the parties.

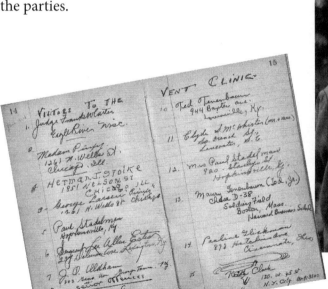

But most importantly, anyone passing through the area was encouraged to stop by Vent Haven to share their latest adventures, view the collection, and enjoy a hot meal with W. S. and his wife Josephine, "Muzz." In 1941, W. S. started a guest book which is part of the collection today.

December 9

It was this month in 1964 that ventriloquial education took a huge leap forward. The Juro Novelty Company released Jimmy Nelson's *Instant Ventriloquism* album. The key to this revolutionary approach was letter substitution.

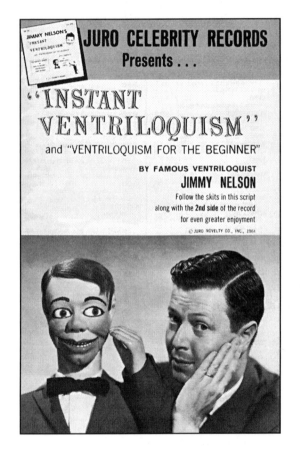

Jimmy's albums taught a whole generation of ventriloquists. To this day, *Instant Ventriloquism* remains the standard for learning ventriloquism. Many of today's greatest ventriloquists received a Danny O'Day dummy and these two albums as Christmas gifts.

(continued)

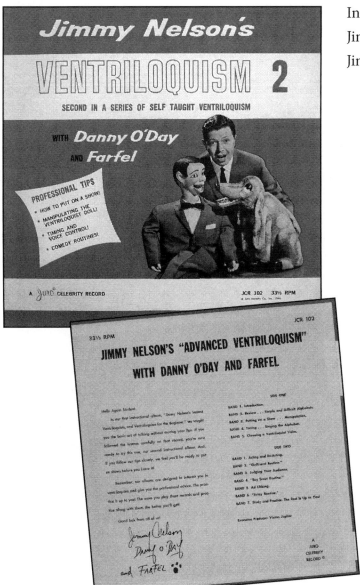

In 1966, Juro Novelty Company released Jimmy's second instructional album, Jimmy Nelson's *Ventriloquism 2*.

Writing about his life, the *New York Times* said, "As successful as Jimmy Nelson was on television and in nightclubs, he had a greater legacy as a ventriloquism teacher, via instructional albums he recorded in the mid-1960s."

December 11

Did you know that today is the birthday of figure maker and vent educator
Clinton Detweiler (December 11, 1936 - January 22, 2013)?

In 1969 Clinton continued the Maher
School of Ventriloquism, a home
study course that taught him the art
of ventriloquism. As a respected
figure maker, Clinton was known for
the ability to make anything talk.
He also published the ventriloquist
newsletter *Newsy Vents*.

December 11

On this day in 1912, figure maker George McElroy was born (December 11, 1912 -December 6, 1997). George, along with older brother Glenn, produced what many have called "the Stradivarius of ventriloquial figures."

While Glenn took care of the mechanics, George was responsible for the modeling, artwork, and painting. The McElroy brothers began making figures for the Abbott's Magic Novelty Company in 1936. It was Percy Abbott who encouraged the McElroys to make vent figures.

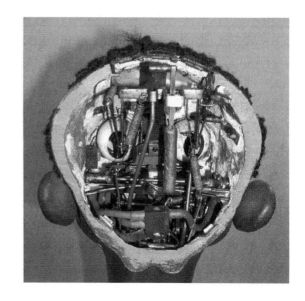

December 12

On this date in 1937, Mae West was banned from radio for 13 years for talking suggestively to a ventriloquist puppet. Mae West appeared on the *The Chase and Sanborn Hour* with Edgar Bergen and Charlie McCarthy. In the flirtatious back and forth, West invites Charlie to her home to play in her "woodpile." Charlie and Ms. West had this conversation:

Charlie: "Not so loud, Mae, not so loud! All my girlfriends are listening."
Mae: "Oh, yeah! You're all wood and a yard long."
Charlie: "Yeah."
Mae: "You weren't so nervous and backward when you came up to see me at my apartment. In fact, you didn't need any encouragement to kiss me."
Charlie: "Did I do that?"
Mae: "Why, you certainly did. I got marks to prove it. An' splinters, too."
(continued)

The FCC deemed the exchange indecent, and West was thereby banned from radio for the next 13 years. However, *The Chase and Sanborn Hour's* ratings had a huge jump as listeners tuned in to hear what might happen next.

December 13

On this day in 1911, the very first motion picture to utilize a ventriloquist theme was released. Called *The Ventriloquist's Trunk* and produced by Vitagraph Company of America, it was a one reel silent slapstick comedy.

The story involves a traveling ventriloquist (Ralph Ince) who arrives at a boarding house, setting up his figures to rehearse. Another guest (Flora Finch) assumes he has brought in non-paying boarders, so he drops his figures out the window in order not to get caught.

December 14

On this day in 1883, Grace Larsen (December 14, 1883 – January 15, 1948) was born. Known as Madam Pinxy, Grace is regarded as the founder of the International Brotherhood of Ventriloquists (IBV). Grace served as secretary of the organization and published the club's magazine, *Grapevine News,* from 1941 through 1944.

December 15

On this day in 1928, the great Jimmy Nelson
(December 15, 1928 - September 24, 2019)
was born in Chicago. In 1937, Jimmy's Aunt
Margaret gifted him his first ventriloquist
dummy, a bingo prize she'd won named
Dummy Dan. Jimmy's indelible contributions
to the art of vent are instructional albums,
superior technique and performance, generosity
of time and goodness of heart.

December 16

It was this week in 1964 that Willie Tyler and Lester recorded their comedy album *hello dummy!*

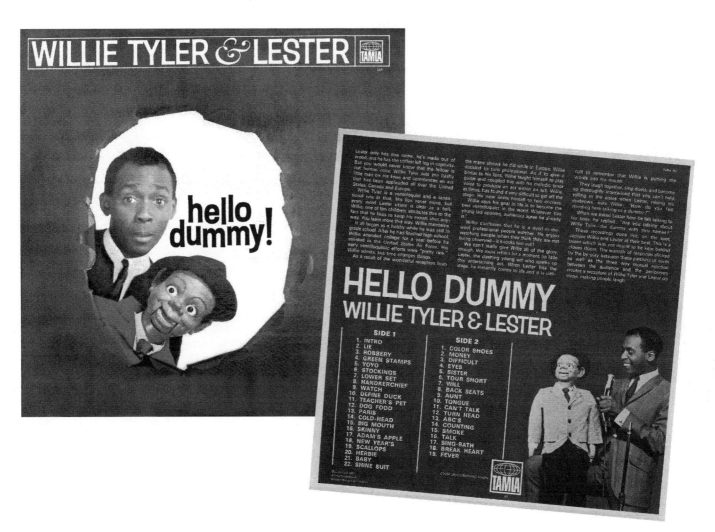

Released on Motown Record's Tamla label, this performance was recorded live at the Fox Theater in Detroit. Willie and Lester were the emcees for Motown's touring show of stars. The Lester pictured on the album cover currently resides at Vent Haven Museum.

December 17

Did you know that today is the anniversary of Edgar Bergen and Charlie McCarthy's appearance on Rudy Vallee's radio show?

Chase & Sanborn present

★ A GREAT NEW ★
VARIETY SHOW
*Starring Sensational Successes
of Stage and Screen*

W. C. FIELDS, EDGAR BERGEN,
DON AMECHE, WERNER JANSSEN
*—and a whole galaxy of Guest
Artists—from Hollywood*
Sponsored by CHASE & SANBORN COFFEE
STATION WSAN—8:00 P. M., E. D. S. T. and every Sunday Night thereafter

*Ventriloquist
of the Air—
Listen and laugh!*

MUSIC! LAUGHTER! HEART THROBS! LISTEN IN!

Two producers saw Bergen and Charlie perform at the Rainbow Room in NYC and recommended them for a guest spot on the 1936 show. They were so successful on the show that the following year they were given regular roles as part of *The Chase and Sanborn Hour*. Charlie and Edgar were on the air over 19 years from May 9, 1937 to July 1, 1956.

December 18

It was on this day in 1951 that Jimmy Nelson became the spokesperson on the *Texaco Star Theater* hosted by Milton Berle. It was Season 4, Episode 14 when Jimmy took over for Sid Stone. Jimmy continued through 1954, performing the live skits and five-minute commercials each week.

December 19

It was tomorrow on December 20, 1944 that
W. S. Berger saw the 19-year-old ventriloquist
Rondelle (McCutty) Favara (March 6, 1925 -
December 1, 2000) perform in Cincinnati.

He became a fan and they communicated throughout her career.
Her partner at the time was a Frank Marshall figure named Jerry.
Rondelle would sing and then Jerry would sing and jump up and
down. In 1965, Rondelle's husband, Louis, created an automated
dummy for her. The puppet rode and steered a tricycle independently and, despite the name Candy Buttons, was male.

December 20

On this day in 1891, ventriloquist and figure maker Fred Henry Koetsch (December 20, 1891 – 1975) was born. Performing as Fred Ketch, he served in World War I and then served with the USO, performing for the troops during World War II.

His partner Jerry would be known as Sergeant Jerry for these performances. A remarkable piece of the act was Jerry playing the mouth harp while Fred sang along. This was achieved through the technique of throat or overtone singing.

December 21

Charlie McCarthy Detective was released tomorrow in 1939. It was the second movie Bergen and McCarthy made for Universal Pictures following *Letter of Introduction.*

Wooden you know it? When Charlie McCarthy and Edgar Bergen attend a party held by a crooked editor, they become thrown into a mystery when their host is killed. With both a reporter and a mobster suspected of murder, Charlie and Edgar try to figure out who done it. But can they solve the case, or will they just look like a couple of dummies?

December 22

On this day in 1922, ventriloquist Paul Winchell (December 22, 1922 – June 24, 2005) was born. His birth name was Paul Wilchinsky and he became television's first great ventriloquial star.

Paul was not only an extremely creative ventriloquist and amazing actor, but was also the voice of Tigger, Baby Smurf, and Dick Dastardly, to name a few. As a child, Paul suffered from polio. He taught himself ventriloquism while he was bedridden.

December 23

Today is ventriloquist Dan Horn's birthday. Known as the "Stand-Up Ventriloquist," Dan has the distinction of being one of the finest practitioners of puppet manipulation. For eight years Dan was a cast member and writer for KPHO unconventional kids' TV series *The Wallace & Ladmo Show* that aired in Arizona from 1954 to 1989.

December 24

Happy Holidays!

December 25

It's a fact that Jeff Dunham began ventriloquism in 1970 at age eight. As a Christmas present, Jeff's parents gave him a Juro Novelty Company Mortimer Snerd puppet and the accompanying how-to album. By the fourth grade, Dunham knew he wanted to be a professional ventriloquist.

December 26

Edgar Bergen was certainly not the first to truly popularize the marketing technique that his wooden partners had a life outside of the act, but he was, without a doubt, the best.

Bergen worked tirelessly to make it appear that Charlie McCarthy was a real little boy. Charlie had his own room in the Bergen house and did many things away from the stage, including going to college, flying, enjoying the beach, and even dating some of his co-stars. Charlie was awarded a degree from Northwestern University in Master of Innuendo and Snappy Comebacks. Charlie received thousands of fan letters per week, illustrating that many of them believed he was a real boy.

December 27

The Vent Haven Museum has approximately 20,000 photos in their library and archives. Founder W. S. Berger would begin most of his vent friendships by sending a photo of himself and requesting a signed photo in return. He would frame the majority of them and he called the photo display his "Gallery of Rogues."

December 28

Phyllis Easley, known as Phyllis Willis, was born two days from now on December 30th. The exact year of her birth is unknown since she put on her International Brotherhood of Ventriloquists' application "30 Dec Over 21" as her birthday. Her signature routine was her partner speaking with famous movie stars over the phone. Phyllis not only spoke for her partner, but impersonated the stars utilizing a classic telephone distant voice.

December 29

Tomorrow is the anniversary of the birth of ventriloquist Richard J. Bruno (December 30, 1903 – May 18, 1986). He used the stage name Dick Bruno and Monsieur Brunard.

MONSIEUR BRUNARD
(The Fabulous Frenchman)
and JOE FLIP
231
213 East 50th Street, NYC-22-N.Y.
Plaza 9-1397

He became Monsieur Brunard when he invented an entirely new stage character that was a sophisticated native Frenchman utilizing a French dialect. A unique element was that his long time puppet partner, Joe Flip, replied with a New York accent. Joe Flip resides at Vent Haven Museum today.

December 30

Today is soft figure maker Verna Finly's birthday. Many ventriloquists and soft puppet makers consider Verna the "Grandmother" of soft puppets. Verna was Mary Ann Taylor's mentor and made soft puppets for many great ventriloquists such as Jeff Dunham and Dale Brown.

Did you know that Verna learned her trade and began her career as a puppet maker and costumer for a children's show? She worked with Jim Henson protégé Bob Elnicky at the ABC affiliate WXYZ in Detroit, Michigan.

December 31

Figure maker Brant Gilmer's birthday is today. Brant is one of the few who hand carve fine wooden ventriloquial figures with multiple animations. Trained as a mechanical engineer, his figures are known and celebrated for their smooth operation. The more complex characters' facial animations result from his design of intricate mechanisms within the heads.

Brant's interest in ventriloquism inspired him, in 1956, to write Vent Haven Museum founder W.S. Berger inquiring about instructional sources for building ventriloquial figures. His resulting creations are owned and used by some of the best ventriloquists in the business.

December 31

The Shari Show premiered on this day at 7:30 PM in 1975 and aired for two seasons. This children's show was later syndicated, running in the afternoons after kids would get home from school. It featured all of Shari's usual partners as well as new ones designed for this show.

With Special Thanks for
Encouragement and Support

Timothy T. Miller

Christopher Lockhart

Donna Jean Simon

Claude Yacoel

Marie and Ryan Northwick

Jimmy Nelson
Betty Nelson

Christopher Alvarado

Mary Alvarado

Jolene Adams
William Gary Richmond

Harry Wiesner

Leslye Hunter

Annie Roberts

Bryan Sweasy

Jay and Sandra Johnson

Kelly Asbury

Dale Brown
Leslie Brown

Dr. Stefan (Stevo) Schüling

Dr. Alan Blumenstyk

Atomic Cherry
John Garvin

Pop Twist Entertainment
Doug Zwick

Sheryl Scarborough
Jerry Piatt

Elliot and Kate Anders

Patricia Calvert

Thomas Ethan Harris

Sue Keenan

Tom Connor

Greg Hurst

Susan Turk

Martha Chavez

Alex Ramirez

Photo Sources

Vent Haven Museum

Tom Ladshaw Collection and Archives

Jay Johnson

Jeff Dunham

Jimmy and Betty Nelson

Alan Cradick

Burt Dubrow

Mallory Lewis

Kathy Bugasky/SIFF

Henrik/SIFF

Kate Anders

Elliot Anders

Montivagus Productions

Bryan W. Simon

Carol Rosseg

Lynn Trefzger

Carla Rhodes

Hanna Toresson

Susan Edwards Martin

Allan Blumenstyk

Ronn Lucas

Norm Nielsen

Otto Petersen

Stevo Schüling

Willie Tyler

Vonda Kay Van Dyke

Matthew Rolston
Pointed Leaf Press

Warner Brothers Television

Warner Brothers Animation

MGM Animation

Saturday Evening Post
May 9, 1953

Popular Mechanics
March 1938

Time
November 20, 1944
May 15, 1950

Flying and Popular Aviation
January 1941

Life

Phil Cho Art

Ealing Studios

Vitaphone Varieties
Vitaphone Studios

Kelly Asbury

Playbill

Terry Fator

Sylvia Cirilo-Fletcher

United Artists

Lions Gate Films

Smith Handerson

Buddy Big Mountain

Jet

Amy Druskovich

MAT Puppets

CBS

DC Comics

American Broadcasting Company (ABC)

National Broadcasting Company (NBC)

Variety

Paramount Pictures

Megan Piphus

Berkley Books

Comedy Central

Twentieth Century Fox Film Corporation

RKO Radio Pictures

FX Television

Vitagraph Company of America

Republic Pictures

Tim Selberg

Columbia Pictures

PBS

Resources

Vent Haven Museum Library and Archives

Tom Ladshaw Collection and Archives

IMDb.com

*Dummy Days: America's Favorite Ventriloquists
From Radio and Early TV*
by Kelly Asbury
Angel City Press

I'm No Dummy
Directed by Bryan W. Simon
Montivagus Productions

A Jimmy Nelson Celebration: 70 Years of Laughter
By Tom Ladshaw

Vent Haven Museum: It's Past, Present, and Future
By Lisa Sweasy

I Can See Your Lips Moving
by Valentine Vox
Players Press

Other Voices: Ventriloquism from B.C to T.V.
by Stanley Burns

Eddie Brandt's Saturday Matinee
North Hollywood, CA

Saturday Evening Post
May 9, 1953

Popular Mechanics
March 1938

Time
November 20, 1944

Flying and Popular Aviation
January 1941

Life

The Oracle

Amy Druskovich
Toni I. Benson Local History and Genealogy Room
Webster Memorial Library
Van Buren District Library, Decatur, Michigan.

All By My Selves: Walter, Peanut, Achmed and Me
By Jeff Dunham
Berkley Press

On the Front Cover

Red Flannels graces the front cover of this book with a wall from Vent Haven Museum in the background.

An extremely expressive Frank Marshall figure, Red Flannels began his residency at Vent Haven in July 1992. His ventriloquist partner was the talented Terry Bennett (April 25, 1930 - October 12, 1977) who, among his many accomplishments, joined the staff of WBKB-channel 7 in Chicago at age 23, where he created, produced, and wrote *Jobblewocky Place*. Airing weekday mornings in 1954, the preschool program introduced his audience to a stable of ventriloquial and hand puppet characters. It was one of the first TV shows to weave eduction and moral lessons into a children's program. It earned three Emmy nominations.

Back Cover Photos
(left to right)

William Wood Poster

Nina Conti & Monk

Jay Johnson & Spaulding

Brenda Barron & Kenny

Ronn Lucas & Buffalo Billy

Paul Winchell & Jerry Mahoney

Jeff Dunham & Partners

Jimmy Nelson, Danny O'Day & Farfel

Cecilia "Zillah" Ustav & Totte

Edgar Bergen & Charlie McCarthy

About the Author

Bryan W. Simon never thought he would direct a movie or write a book about ventriloquism. A screenwriters' strike changed all that, inspiring him to rediscover an art form that reawakened his inner child. An award-winning and critically acclaimed director, writer, and visualist, Simon's feature films include the smash hit comedy documentary *I'm No Dummy*, the first feature length film on ventriloquism; the big screen adaptation of the Tony® Award winning Broadway show, *Jay Johnson: The Two & Only!*; and the indie darling, *Along For The Ride*. He has written articles on filmmaking for *MovieMaker* magazine, *No Film School*, *The Wrap*, and others. He has been a guest instructor in directing and filmmaking at various universities and colleges and was the co-producer of the educational seminar series at the American Cinematheque in Hollywood. In addition, Bryan was the Founder and Artistic Director for the Chicago area Stage Two Theatre Company. Bryan and his wife, film producer Marjorie Engesser, proudly serve on the Vent Haven Museum Board of Advisors.

Visit his website at: *www.bryanwsimon.com*

Made in the USA
Columbia, SC
13 June 2021